Live Free
and
Eat Pie!

A Storyteller's Guide to New Hampshire

Also from Islandport Press

Billy Boy by Jean Mary Flahive

My Life in the Maine Woods by Annette Jackson

Contentment Cove by Miriam Colwell

Young by Miriam Colwell

Stealing History by William D. Andrews

Shoutin' into the Fog by Thomas Hanna

down the road a piece: A Storyteller's Guide to Maine by John McDonald

A Moose and a Lobster Walk into a Bar by John McDonald

Windswept by Mary Ellen Chase

Mary Peters by Mary Ellen Chase

Silas Crockett by Mary Ellen Chase

Nine Mile Bridge by Helen Hamlin

In Maine by John N. Cole

The Cows Are Out! by Trudy Chambers Price

Hauling by Hand by Dean Lawrence Lunt

At One: In a Place Called Maine by Lynn Plourde and Leslie Mansmann

The Little Fisherman by Margaret Wise Brown and Dahlov Ipcar

Titus Tidewater by Suzy Verrier

A is for Acadia by Richard Johnson and Ruth Gortner Grierson

These and other Maine books are available at:
www.islandportpress.com

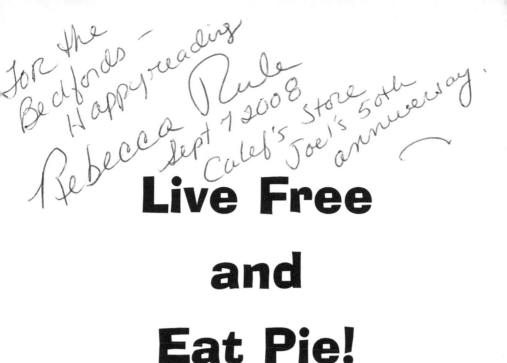

For the Bedfords — Happy reading
Rebecca Rule
Sept 7 2008
Caleb's Store
Joel's 50th anniversary.

Live Free
and
Eat Pie!

A Storyteller's Guide to New Hampshire

by Rebecca Rule

ISLANDPORT PRESS

ISLANDPORT PRESS • FRENCHBORO • YARMOUTH

Islandport Press
P.O. Box 10
Yarmouth, Maine 04096

www.islandportpress.com

ISBN: 978-1-934031-17-9
Library of Congress Control Number: 2008928221

First edition published June 2008

Book design by Michelle Lunt / Islandport Press
Cover Design by Karen Hoots / Mad Hooter Design

Dedication

To Phil and Diane from New Boston, friends who love to laugh. When I see you in the audience I know it's going to be a good night!

And to all the folks who show up at my gigs ready to listen, laugh, and maybe share a story or two.

A storyteller without an audience is talking to herself.

Acknowledgments

Record fish figures came from the New Hampshire Fish and Game Department (www.wildlife.state.nh.us). Thanks, Jane Vachon, for keeping me up to date on this.

Amanda Grady, public policy director, and Jennifer Devarie, public policy specialist, both on the staff of the New Hampshire Coalition Against Domestic and Sexual Violence, provided legislative gems from their collection of quotes from lawmakers, including the quote about the Baby Jesus from Sen. Jack Barnes. Thanks, Amanda and Jennifer!

Thanks to Jennie Brown of Berlin for the Ozzie Wheeler story and others.

Thanks to Ada and Urban Hatch and the Hatchlings for many great stories. Even though they're set in Maine, they can be adapted for New Hampshire. Don't tell anybody.

My friend Pauline Dupuis taught me to make meat pie, but I didn't include the recipe here—just the vague ingredients—because it's a secret! Thanks, Pauline. We love the meat pie.

Howard Odell and Buddy McDougall sat with me at Friendly's one afternoon and told many stories, including the one about Hattie and the Party Line. Thanks, boys.

Daniel Webster Harvey and Harvey Tolman—thanks for your stories. They could fill a whole book!

Thanks to all those who've shared stories with me and their neighbors at my "Evenings of Yankee Humor" and "Better Than a Poke in the Eye" performances, often sponsored by the New

Hampshire Humanities Council. I don't know all your names, but I do my best to remember your stories and pass them on.

Thanks to K. Seavey for cheerfully shoveling the driveway while I was working on this book.

Adi Rule inspires me with her wicked sense of humor every day.

Thanks to Bud and Jean Barker, my parents, for telling stories all the time and teaching me that life is one long story, more funny than not.

John Rule, thanks for all the research and proofreading, and also for putting up with me for 33 years (so far).

Table of Contents

ix

Just who the heck does Becky Rule think she is?

I was born in Concord in 1954 (which almost makes me a New Hampshire native) to parents Jean and Lewis Barker, who were born in Danbury (which almost makes them natives, too). I grew up on Corn Hill Road in Boscawen, where, at the age of six I began keeping a little notebook of funny sayings. My first was: "Hs brans ratl arond lik bbs in a bxcr," which translates to: "His brains rattle around like beebees in a boxcar." I think my dad said it to my Uncle Fred about a mutual acquaintance who was none too bright. I've been writing funny things down ever since.

This urge to write things down took me to, where else, the University of New Hampshire. Then to graduate school for, what else, fiction writing, at where else, UNH. I taught writing for a decade or two at, where else, UNH. I also taught business writing for a couple of years, but that gave me a headache. Meantime, I married a funny man named John Rule. I call him John Rule. We had a daughter named Adi Rule. I call her Adi Rule. They amuse me endlessly.

Over the years, I wrote freelance articles and short stories. Oh, and book reviews. I've written, to date, almost 700 book reviews. That's a lot! I've been writing three or four a month since 1992. It adds up.

That's right, I've never had a real job. Just lucky, I guess.

At some point, 'round about menopause, I started telling stories to anybody who would listen. At first I was reading

Thirty-five years ago, a couple moved into a small town with their six children. At that time, the population happened to be 800, so the dad—who told me this story—figured they'd increased it by 1 percent. He was pretty proud of that.

At the village store, he introduced himself to a native, who said: "I know who you are. You're the new people."

"That's right," the dad said.

"We just built a new school," the native said. "And we don't want to build another."

Which was just his way of saying: "Welcome to New Hampshire."

from my collection of short stories—*The Best Revenge*—and telling funny stories about the stories in between reading the stories. Then I figured out that telling stories was a lot more fun than reading them. Also, my bifocals needed updating and you know how expensive glasses are. So I let go of the pages and started looking at audiences. They looked back at me. (All except the New England Handspinners Association; those ladies didn't look up once. They spun and knit. I talked. They did laugh from time to time, which was reassuring.)

After a while, *New Hampshire Magazine* dubbed me, "Thalia: the Muse of Comedy." Thank you very much. I've never been referred to as a Greek goddess before. Over time, that title morphed into "The Muse of Humor." One fellow with a lisp introduced me as "The Moose of Humor," a title I've embraced ever since, though I have no antlers and weigh less than the average 1,000-pound *Antilocapra americana*. (That means moose.) Also, I'm not quite 6 feet at the shoulder, and usually get fewer than ten Ixodidae (ticks) per year instead of the 55,000, give or take, carried by your average *Antilocapra americana*.

You got to hand it to moose: they're so homely it's humorous. We have a lot of them in New Hampshire, so I figured I might as well join the herd.

Long story long, for the last decade or so, I've been making tracks all over the state telling and collecting stories. "That reminds me of a story," somebody will say, and we're off! Telling stories in Salisbury, Peterborough, Canterbury, Stratford, and Strafford, I'll say: "If you tell me a story, I'll make a note of it in this little book, and maybe tell it in the next town." Only one person, in hundreds of performances, has ever said *Don't do it.*

"I'll tell you a story," this lady said, "but don't you go retelling it. I'm saving it for my memoir!"

Fair enough.

Most people seem to appreciate having their stories collected and retold. A good story lives on and on. It may change some in passing, but the essence remains. When I was performing at the Franklin Opera House, my daughter overheard a guy in the row ahead say to his friend: "I think this is my story coming up."

Like Big Mouth Billy Bass, the singing wall plaque, stories are meant to be regifted. You give your story to me and I pass it on. Each teller spins it his or her own way, like politicians do. Some stories turn into folklore. I call them *apocryphal*, which means they may have been true once, but over time have taken on shapes and truths all their own. In other words, they are big, fat, wonderful lies. You know, like the one about the farmer relieved to learn the homestead he'd lived in all his life was actually in New Hampshire, not Maine: "Couldn't stand another one of those Maine winters," he famously says.

I don't tell these apocryphal stories very often. Don't have to. In any given performance, somebody will rise from the audience to regale us, saying: "This is a true story. It really happened to my Cousin Pod a couple years ago in Westmoreland. You see, Pod had this three-legged pig named Charity. She was an amazing pig."

"How's that?"

"One time Pod's John Deere tipped over and Pod's left leg was caught underneath, pinned up against a rock. That pig come running, and with her snout and front legs, she dug all around that rock and that caught leg and freed him."

"That's amazing!"

"Another time, a bad fella tried to break into the house. Pod didn't wake up, but Charity did. She had him down and cornered in the door yard. Pod heard all the squealing, woke up, and called the police. Charity kept that bad fella in custody until Chief Harvey came to haul him away.

"And when the barn caught fire, that pig herded the cows to safety, and took a litter of kittens out by the napes of their necks, two at a time."

"So how did she lose her leg?"

"Well, a good pig like that, you don't eat all at once."

I often tell a couple of true Wolfeboro stories. The first came from a lawyer who explained that the Wolfeboro Airport was kind of a small operation, run for years by Merwyn Horne and his wife, Eleanor. One day the lawyer called Merwyn up on the phone. "Merwyn," he said, "I got a friend flying in from New York State later today. When he lands, is there a phone he can call me up on so I can come down and pick him up?"

"Yuh," Merwyn said, monotone, "I'm talking on it."

Undeterred, the lawyer pressed on. "The other thing is, Merwyn, I understand you close up shop at five o'clock every day."

"That's right," Merwyn said.

"Well, I don't know as my friend will get into town before five o'clock. What if he flies in at five-thirty or six? What happens after five o'clock?"

Merwyn said, "Not a hell of a lot."

Wolfeboro Airport always was tricky to fly into, situated on the shore of Lake Winnipesaukee. If you overshot the runway, you'd end up in the drink. When I announced at a performance that I had a Wolfeboro Airport story to tell, a man said, "I bet I know it."

"How would you know that?" I asked.

" 'Cause I told it to you a year ago."

"Why don't you tell it?" I said.

"No," he said. "I want to hear you tell it."

So I did.

When I got to the end, I said, "Did I get it right?"

He said, "No."

In the months since he'd told me the story, the details had changed. I didn't do it on purpose. It's just that stories . . . evolve. Here's my wrong version of a true Wolfeboro Airport story:

So this fella was flying into the Wolfeboro Airport in a two-seater plane. He was the passenger and he was a little nervous, because he happened to know Merwyn closed up shop at five o'clock on weekdays. Here it was the middle of the night, almost nine-thirty. He said to the pilot: "Is it a problem that Merwyn closes up shop at five?"

"Not really," the pilot said. "The only thing is, when Merwyn shuts the place down at five, he turns all the lights out. But don't worry. My wife knows we're coming. She'll drive the Studebaker to the end of the runway and shine the lights so we can see to land."

"Isn't that a little dangerous?" the passenger said.

"No," the pilot said. "Well, it is a little more dangerous then it used to be. Since she filed for divorce."

Anyway, in my travels as a storyteller, I can't claim to have visited every town in New Hampshire, but pretty close. In Plainfield, a woman told of a couple who married in their seventies. When the minister asked the groom to repeat after him, "I vow to live with Matilda in peace and unity," the groom retorted, "I'll vow to live in peace but damned if I'll live in Unity." Unity is the next town over.

A few weeks later, I told the story in Unity.

Often I tell stories at historical societies or libraries. Different groups hire me—like county farm bureaus and the New England Breeders of Elk and Deer. The latter was a lively evening that included an auction. I was the auctioneer, and things were going right along smooth, until I got to the certificate for elk semen donated by Charlie Pickering. "Who will bid a hundred dollars for Charlie Pickering's semen?" I called out. The young lady bartender did a double take. But the elk and deer breeders were uncowed. As I recall, Charlie's semen sold for about $400.

Oh yes, I'm out and about. I've included a lot of stories in this book because a surefire way to get to know a place is through its stories. And, as I've lived in New Hampshire all my life (so far), over the years I've picked up a few tidbits about navigating my home state that I'm happy to pass on. But remember, I'm a storyteller. In other words, a professional liar. As my father always says: "Why tell the truth when a lie will do just as well and be a lot more interesting?"

So take the advice in this guide to the Granite State with few grains of road salt. And if you should find yourself on a slick, winding road when the salt trucks are out in force, please remember: Bridges freeze first.

Startin' Out
New Hampshire in Brief

Whether you've just flown in from a flat spot like
Iowa, traveled by train from a crowded burg like New York
City, or drifted down from an exotic country like Canada or
Maine; whether you're visiting for a weekend, a summer, or
you've lived here for a decade or two, welcome to New
Hampshire.

You probably already know this, but New Hampshire is
small, smaller than 45 of the 50 states. Smaller than Vermont
by a smidge, but bigger than New Jersey, Connecticut,
Delaware, and Rhode Island. Alaska's about 60 times the size of
New Hampshire, but how many sugar maples do they have in
Juneau, huh? How many gallons of maple syrup do those
Eskimos produce, huh? Just saying.

New Hampshire's population of over a million and a quarter, give or take, is quite pale— 95 percent white, they say. And
in winter, we're apt to get even paler from hunkering down by
the woodstove during cold snaps—like January. The U.S.
Census calculates that New Hampshire has 137.8 people per
square mile, but that's just silly. In the square mile around my
house in Northwood, I count . . . well, I never counted, but it's
considerably less than 137.8.

Maybe it's an exaggeration to say everybody in New
Hampshire knows everybody else. But the truth is, live here

1

At one New Hampshire sap house, a lady from away, looking at the boiling sap, commented on its clear color. "I always thought maple syrup was brown," she said to the farmer.

"Ma'am," the farmer said, "you must be thinking of Vermont maple syrup."

long enough, and most of the ones you're not related to, you'll at least recognize by sight.

We're a small state, but full. Full of people in big cities like Manchester, Portsmouth, and Nashua all situated in what we call the Deep South. In the true North Country, we're talking Coos County, some square miles are home to more deer, moose, mountain lions, sidehill wampuses, and bear than people, which is just how the North Country folks like it. On average and taken as a whole, New Hampshire is full of trees, full of pep, and full of exciting attractions like the Anheuser-Busch Brewery in Merrimack, where you can enjoy a free tour and a beer; Santa's Village in Jefferson, where the jolly old elf himself summers along with his entourage; or America's Stonehenge in Salem, mysterious rock structures inscribed with writings that might be Ogham, Phoenician, or Iberian Punic. That's right, Iberian Punic. America's Stonehenge could have been built by Abenakis, Vikings, or, most likely, space aliens. The tour is self-guided and no pets allowed, but watch out for the eight resident alpacas.

General activities

New Hampshire is full of a variety of tourist hot spots. It's also likely to be full of tourists—every season but mud—looking for opportunities to:

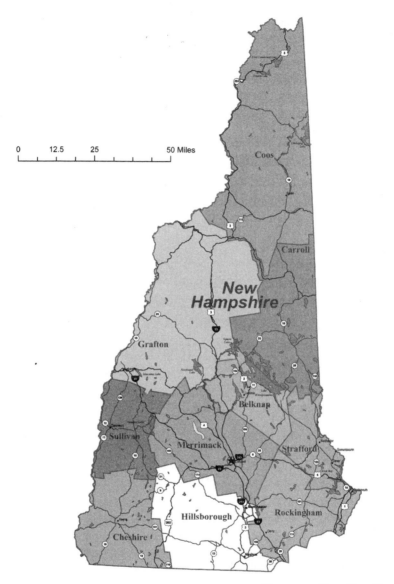

Map courtesy of Digital Vector Maps

New Hampshire, from the North Country to the Deep South, comprises ten counties, each distinct in their own peculiar ways.

3

Climb a mountain

We've got 48 over 4,000 feet and a bunch of stubby ones, too, including Monadnock, the most-climbed mountain in the world. Used to be Fuji, in Japan, but we passed their record, last count.

Ski down a mountain

Best attempted in winter. Most of them have tows and a good many have snow, December through spring melt, depending on the year.

Take a dip in the Atlantic

In high summer—which lasts a day and a half—the water temperature at Hampton Beach can reach a toasty 68 degrees. Most of the year, it's closer to 45, what we call refreshing!

Fish, boat, or swim

New Hampshire is the land of 1,000 lakes and ponds. Well, actually it's 975, but I rounded up. **Tip:** In New Hampshire lakes are generally bigger than ponds, unlike Maine where the opposite is often true. Contrary buggers. If Huron, Superior and Michigan were in Maine, they'd call them the Great Ponds. In New Hampshire, if the word lake comes first, as in Lake Winnipesaukee, the body of water is apt to be particularly large.

Shop

Outlets abound, with more than 60 in North Conway (Route 16) and around 50 in Tilton (Exit 20 off 93). Stuff at those outlets is so cheap, even I buy it. Last year I bought two pairs of shoes, just alike except one pair was brown and one black. I can only wear one pair at a time, so two seemed wasteful, but heck, the checkout lady practically paid me to take them away. And, get this: NO SALES TAX!

Interact with natives

We're friendlier than we look. But you will have to initiate conversation. We don't.

Take a picture of a moose or a presidential candidate

Every four years, during primary season, the presidential candidates are, in fact, thicker than ticks on a moose's back.

Listen

To the eerie calls of the loons and assess their platforms.

New Hampshire ain't Vermont, and it ain't Maine neither

To the fellow from away who asks: "Aren't New Hampshire, Vermont, and Maine pretty much the same?" I raise my eyebrows real high and say: "Uh, no."

Mainers, Vermonters, and New Hampshirites know that our three states are as different as lobster, cheddar cheese, and granite. We have about as much in common as rock snot, zucchini, and William Loeb. That is, some, but not a lot.

Maine and Vermont are nice enough, I guess, if you like potatoes or Green Mountain Boys. But New Hampshire's got the White Mountains (high) and Hampton Beach (wet). We got the Mount Washington Hotel (elegant) and Wentworth-by-the-Sea (also elegant but with less elevation). We got Dartmouth College (prestigious) and the Atlantic Culinary Academy in Dover (good cooks). We got J.D. Salinger and P.J. O'Rourke (good writers). Supreme Court Justice David Souter hails from

5

Weare. (He's smart.) Actress and writer Sarah Silverman hails from Manchester. (She's smart and funny.)

We talk different, too, which I'll explain later. But for now, it's enough to know that the native New Hampshire accent, and its variations, combines the dropped Rs of the Maine accent, and the stretched As of Massachusetts with a touch of the "oi" from Vermont or, possibly, upstate New York (transferred during the Great Migration of 1884) that creeps into words like fine (foine) and mine (moine).

Some people say to me: "What is that accent you have?"

I say, "New Hampshire."

They say (because they don't know any better), "We didn't realize people from New Hampshire had accents."

I say, "New Hampshire is sandwiched between Maaaasachusetts (think Kennedy), Vermont (think Fred Tuttle and his Holstein kews) and Maine (think Bert and I); how could we not?"

Sure, New Hampshire has a few things in common with our neighbors, like six months of winter and a month of blackflies, but we also claim the only First-in-the-Nation Primary. And we're never going to give that up. They will have to rip that primary from our cold dead hands.

New Hampshire is unique. And it's home. Come home with me—by reading this book, I mean—and I'll show you around. Let's go!

1

Basics

If you show up at a New Hampshirite's house and he's expecting you, the traditional warm greeting is "Where the hell you been?" If you show up at his house and he's *not* expecting you, the traditional warm greeting is, "What the hell you doing here?"

For us in New Hampshire, it's all a matter of interpretation. That being said, there are a few givens that will help you during your stay with us. Here are some definitions you can count on:

New Hampshirite—Someone who lives in New Hampshire.

Native—Someone who can claim five generations in the ground.

Transplant—Someone from another place who makes the wise choice to live in New Hampshire.

Summer person—Someone from away who enjoys our glorious New Hampshire summers but bugs out when the going gets tough.

Away—Any place that is not here.

Leaf peeper—Someone from away who drives through during foliage season to look at the changing leaves.

Yankee—Well, it depends. The definition of *Yankee* may be traced to Mark Twain (*A Connecticut Yankee in King Arthur's Court*), but it has been refined by Jud Hale of *Yankee* magazine, a man who's done a lot of thinking about what it means to be

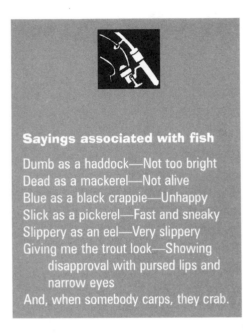

Sayings associated with fish

Dumb as a haddock—Not too bright
Dead as a mackerel—Not alive
Blue as a black crappie—Unhappy
Slick as a pickerel—Fast and sneaky
Slippery as an eel—Very slippery
Giving me the trout look—Showing
    disapproval with pursed lips and
    narrow eyes
And, when somebody carps, they crab.

Yankee. According to Jud and others, to somebody in Europe, a Yankee is an American. To someone who lives south of the Mason-Dixon line, a Yankee is someone who lives north of the Mason-Dixon line. To someone who lives north of the Mason-Dixon line, a Yankee is someone from New England. To people in Rhode Island, Connecticut and Massachusetts, a Yankee is someone from Maine, New Hampshire, or Vermont. To people in Maine, New Hampshire, and Vermont, a Yankee is someone who eats pie for breakfast.

Flatlander—Well, it depends. For many in Maine, Vermont, and New Hampshire, a flatlander is someone from Rhode Island, Connecticut, or Massachusetts. For those in New Hampshire who live in the White Mountains Region, a flatlander is anyone who lives south of the Notches. And for those hardy few who man the weather observatory on top of Mount Washington—the tallest peak in the northeastern U.S., known for having the worst weather in the world—a flatlander is everybody else.

Scissorbeak—A flatlander with an attitude.

8

New Hampshire, the Uzbekistan of New England

The second-best way to know a state, besides stories, is through statistics and facts. Or maybe not. Truth is, statistics lie as much as storytellers. But sometimes it's interesting to see how one place—in this case, the Granite State—measures up to some other place, like, for instance, Uzbekistan.

* Uzbekistan used to be part of the Soviet Union. New Hampshire used to be part of Massachusetts. Eerie, huh?
* Uzbekistan is a landlocked country in Central Asia. New Hampshire boasts 13 miles on the Atlantic in North America.
* The capital of Uzbekistan is Taskent, with a population of 2.1 million. The capital of New Hampshire is Concord, with a population of 52,000.
* Uzbekistan occupies over 172,000 square miles. New Hampshire occupies under 10,000 square miles.
* In 2007, Uzbekistanis used 3.7 million cell phones. That's not so many considering the population is nearly 28 million. That's like one cell phone for every 7.567568 people. With a population of 1,314,895, New Hampshire has, last count, 1,314,895 cell phone users. Even Grammie has gone wireless.

"Hello, Grammie, is that you?"

"Hello?"

"How's the bursitis?"

"What?"

"How's the bur-site-iss?"

"It's not my birthday, is it?"

"Did you see a doctor yet?"

"Dog to the vet? I don't have a dog."

9

The problem is: The White Mountains. Those tall boys raise the devil with reception, especially if you're in a hole.
- Uzbekistan has 12 provinces. New Hampshire has 10 counties.
- In Uzbekistan one in three people is under the age of 14. In New Hampshire one in five people is over the age of 55, and we ain't getting any younger or any less particular.

So, what do Uzbekistan and New Hampshire have in common? Not much. Except weather. Both Uzbekistan and New Hampshire are hot in the summer and cold in the winter. Hey, come January and 30-below, we all put our long johns on one leg at a time.

Buy the numbers

How many moose in Coos County, you ask? How cold does it get on top of Mount Washington in January? How many gallons of sap does it take to make a gallon of maple syrup? How many New Hampshire legislators does it take to screw in a lightbulb? This is New Hampshire by the numbers. You can buy them or not. I'm skeptical myself.

1,314,895   The population of New Hampshire according to the latest census, which is outdated the minute it's printed.

270,000   The average number of anglers who fish our inland waters in a year.

55,000   Average number of ticks on a moose's back. Some have as few as 10,000. Some as many as 120,000. Depends on the moose and its personal hygiene.

10

12,000	Miles of brooks, streams, and rivers. We have no creeks, no cricks, no rivulets, or bayous. And as far as I can tell, a brook and a stream are the same thing. We also have swamps, marshes, bogs, and meadows (swamps, but not so wet). And lately, we've got wetlands, which, as far as I can tell, means swamp, marsh, bog, or meadow, only with more ecological sensitivity. The same thing happened to dumps. We used to have dumps. Now we have Transfer Stations and Waste Management Facilities. This keeps up they'll have to change Tadadump Road in Holderness to Tada-transfer-recycling-waste-management-facility Road.
8,968 or 9,304	Square miles in the state of New Hampshire, depending on who you ask—it's pretty well established that the state is 190 miles long at the long part, 70 miles wide at the fat part.
6,500	Moose in New Hampshire. Approximately. In the late 1800s and early 1900s, the population had dwindled to fewer than 20. (Too many farms, not enough woods, too much hunting.) As the farms died out and the farmers migrated west, the woods took over the old fields, making moose happy. They were also quite pleased by the hunting ban that lasted from 1901 until the 1980s.
975	Lakes and ponds. Or 1,300, depending on whose statistics you read. Must be the 975 counts the big ones, and the 1,300 counts anything bigger than a puddle.
424	Legislators. We have the third-largest legislative body in the English-speaking world, 400 in the

House of Representatives and 24 in the Senate.
That's one legislator for about every 3,000 people, too many for the legislator to know everybody by name, but everybody sure knows their
elected officials, and where they live. Numbers
one and two, as far as massive legislative bodies
go, are the U.S. House of Representatives and the
British Parliament. We pay our legislators $100
per year, plus mileage. So they make out pretty
good, especially the ones from Pittsburg.

274   Islands in Lake Winnipesaukee.

231   Miles per hour; that is, the highest wind speed ever
recorded at ground level anywhere in the world,
on Mount Washington on April 12, 1934. Alex
McKenzie, who was hunkered down on top of the
mountain at the time, observing the weather, is said
to have remarked: "That was quite a puff."

221   Towns.

137.8   People per square mile—but you've got to consider location. On the Everett Turnpike near
Nashua at rush hour, it's more like 5,000 per
square mile, all traveling between 78 and 85 miles
per hour and passing each other on both sides. In
the Great North Woods in April, it's more like
one lost hiker per square mile, sorry he ever left
Massachusetts to find himself by communing with
nature in the season of rebirth and mud.

106   Highest temperature recorded in state in Nashua,
July 4, 1911. That was a scorcher, meaning too
hot even to sit under an awning and watch the
parade.

48   Mountains over 4,000 feet high. The highest is, of
            course, Mount Washington at 6,288 feet. The
            puniest is Mount Isolation at 4,004. I wouldn't
            bother with that one, except if you climb them
            all, you can join the 4000 Footer Club. If you
            climb them all in winter, even better. If you climb
            them all in winter wearing sandals and a sun-
            dress, you can get a 10 percent discount on frost-
            bite treatment at Littleton Hospital.

46   How New Hampshire ranks in size compared to
            the rest of the states. We're about the size and
            shape of Vermont, except Vermont is upside
            down and backwards.

46   Make that MINUS 46, as in 46 below 0. The lowest
            temperature in New Hampshire, recorded on
            January 28, 1925, in Pittsburg. Cold enough for ya?

40   The number of gallons of sap it takes to make a
            gallon of maple syrup.

22   Unincorporated places. They exist but not much
            goes on. Nobody lives there, or if they do, they
            keep a real low profile. Not much nightlife either,
            unless you count the owls. Still, the taxes are rea-
            sonable.

13   Miles of seacoast. Bustling with business and sun-
            and sea-seekers in July and August. In the winter,
            it's hard to find a hot dog or a fried clam there, but
            wonderful for parking and walking nearly deserted
            beaches. Talk about brisk! The wind off the Atlantic
            will cut right through you—in a good way.

2 lbs., 12.8 oz Weight of the biggest black crappie caught in a
            New Hampshire pond. This one was caught in the

Bellamy Reservoir in Madbury by Tom Noyes on February 9, 2000.

11   Lakes and ponds in the town of Wakefield, the most for one town in the state.

10   Counties. Belknap, Carroll, Cheshire, Coos, Grafton, Hillsborough, Merrimack, Rockingham, Strafford, and Sullivan.

9   New Hampshire was the ninth of the original 13 colonies.

3.1   Average high temperature on top of Mount Washington for the month of January 2004. Of course, that high temperature was skewed by the fact that, according to the National Oceanic and Atmospheric Administration, January 13 through 16 that year was particularly cool, with low temperatures from -44 to a sultry -41 degrees Fahrenheit. On the 16th, when the wind picked up, the wind chill reached -101. We call that nippy.

1   Moose of Humor, that's me!

0   Sales tax! It just wouldn't be polite to take advantage of tourists, nice enough to visit our humble state, by imposing a sales tax. Besides, no sales tax cuts down on the math at checkout. In New Hampshire, the amount on the price tag is the actual amount you pay. Ain't that a concept?

Wildlife

New Hampshire's woods are full of animals, and I'm not talking about hunters from out of state.

Moose

Moose, also called Rats of the North Country, are our largest mammal. A bull can go 1,500 pounds, but move silently through the woods—there one minute, gone the next, and the only proof a moose was ever present, a steaming pile of moose beans.

Several North Country companies offer moose tours—by bus, bike, canoe, kayak, on foot, on snowshoes. But you can see moose on your own if you know where to find them—which is most everywhere. They come to the roadsides in winter at dawn and dusk for the road salt. Locals consider them pests because of their tendency to stand in the road in the dark and wreck cars. It's not the speed limits or beefed-up law enforcement that keeps people driving slow on North Country roads, it's the moose.

Road signs in the North Country used to list the number of moose collisions —like McDonald's used to list the number of burgers served. Now, the signs are more general: GAZILLIONS OF COLLISIONS. So slow down and keep your eyeballs peeled, especially in spring, summer, and fall, in the mornings and at dusk, and most especially at night. And, if as you're speeding through the darkness, you should see a big black wall smack in the headlights with knobby knees about eye level, hit the frickin' brakes.

You're more likely to see large numbers of moose around Gorham, Bretton Woods, Colebrook, and destinations north. But they're all over the state. Those long legs carry them great distances. I saw one on a rainy night traveling Route 9 to Keene, way down south. I told my husband to slow down. A

15

car was pulled over beside the road and someone was waving a flashlight. "What the heck?"

John slowed way down. I looked past him, out the side window, and saw knees. Knobby moose knees. We'd missed that bugger by a foot.

New Hampshire's moose hunting season lasts about a week in October. The state workers count up the moose and decide how many need to be "culled." Then they hold a lottery to see which lucky hunters get to do the culling. The lottery winners pay for a permit, go out and find a moose, and shoot it. Sometimes they stuff the heads and hang them on the wall. Sometimes they tan the skin and make moose items out of it, like slippers or chaps. As for the meat, somebody eats it. Either the hunter, or if the hunter doesn't like moose, some lucky recipient, maybe a food bank or soup kitchen. It's sure not to get wasted.

Moose hunting is prohibited the rest of the year. But sometimes folks with empty freezers ignore the law and shoot one anyway. Same with deer. But if you get caught—Big Trouble.

White-tailed deer

When a white-tailed deer is spooked, it jumps, runs, and raises its tail just like a flag, showing the white underside. To spook a deer is called *to jump it*. And the raised white tail is called a *flag*. These are technical hunting terms.

The white-tailed deer is much smaller than the moose, under four feet at the shoulder and weighing between 50 and 250 pounds. While more moose live northerly, more deer live southerly. They like the warm weather and shopping malls. Like moose, the males grow antlers that they shed in late winter and grow again, even bigger the next time.

16

Like moose, they eat twigs, buds, bark, and leaves—small succulent greens. Moose will also eat water plants. They'll wade into the pond and come up with a snoutful. Deer don't go for water plants. Deer do like gardens and will do a number on your corn patch.

Deer hunting is a major New Hampshire sport. The season lasts from September through December, though the

Julie brought her new husband home to New Hampshire to spend time with the family. Touring Colebrook, the new husband had a comment on the big animal standing in the middle of the field. "That's the ugliest horse I ever saw," he said. "You goddamn fool," Uncle Chet said from the backseat. "That's a moose."

weapons change. At first you can only shoot them with bows and arrows. Then muzzleloaders. Then rifles. It's quite a science. Especially figuring out when and where you can shoot deer with antlers vs. deer with no antlers, aka, baldheaded deer. This varies from county to county, and if you're trailing a deer, you might follow him from one county to another and not even realize it.

Nevertheless, hunters manage to figure out the changing regulations each year. In 2007, they bagged over 13,000 deer. Each year they also manage to shoot a hunter or two. This is hard to understand since hunters, even hunters in camouflage hiding in bushes, look nothing like white-tailed deer.

Nonhunters are not advised to walk in the woods during hunting season, unless they're wearing blaze orange and ringing a cowbell. It's scary out there. One time, wearing blaze orange but having left our cowbell at home, my dog Bob and I stumbled into a deer. The deer stared at us. We stared at the deer.

17

Then my survival instinct kicked in: *Hit the deck*. I didn't want us to get caught in the line of fire.

Another time, same woods, same Bob, we looked down the hill and saw a hunter in camouflage tiptoeing among the trees, his muzzleloader at the ready.

"Hey," I yelled.

He jumped!

"I'm not a deer," I yelled. And laughed, a little.

He was not amused. Especially when Bob ran down and jumped all over him, just saying hello but leaving his dog scent all over the poor hunter's pants.

Blackfly

There is an old New Hampshire saying: "If it wa'n't for the blackflies, everybody would want to live here." It just might be true. The Latin name for the two prominent varieties of blackfly in New Hampshire are *Prosimulium mixtum*, which means "vicious, bloodsucking pain in the neck," and *Simulium venustum*, which means "similar but from Venus." Some believe the blackfly is the New Hampshire state bird. It's not. It's Maine's state bird.

Only the females bite. The males just hang around and buzz.

They breed in clean, running water. A polluted brook won't support a healthy blackfly population.

They like dark colors better than light.

They're bigger than no-see-ums, smaller than mosquitoes, and more annoying than telemarketers.

Some scientists believe they swarm your head because they like the carbon dioxide in your breath. Minty mouthwash doesn't seem to fool them.

They don't bite inside a house or inside a car.

They don't bite at night.

They don't bite Libertarians, but they chew the heck out of Democrats.

The bites hurt, but not as much as a mosquito bite or a deerfly bite, or a greenhead bite, or a wasp sting. With blackflies, it's the humming and swarming that will drive you crazy.

Some people swell up from blackfly bites, especially early in the season before your body adjusts. Same thing with the heat. You know how a hot spring day feels hotter than the same hotness would in August? That's because your blood's still thick from winter. Medical fact.

A good stiff breeze will blow blackflies away.

You can't get Lyme disease from blackflies. You get Lyme disease from deer ticks.

Bear

The black bear is native to New Hampshire. A big male can weigh 250 pounds. They are called black bears because of their color. A wild black bear has never killed a person in New Hampshire. They could, but they choose not to. If you meet one in the woods, be afraid. Leave the bear alone and she'll probably leave you alone. Never get between a mother bear and her cubs, or you might end up a statistic.

In fact, bears hear you coming a mile away. Even bear hunters hardly ever see them. I can't remember ever seeing a bear up close in the woods in New Hampshire. Once I saw one run across the road in the distance, but that was about it.

Wild boar

We can thank rich people for the wild boar population in New Hampshire. Corbin Park in Croydon and surrounding towns was established in 1890 as a private hunting preserve.

19

Folks paid, and still pay, good money to belong to the club and earn the privilege of shooting animals within the fences that surround the 24,000 acres. If you don't belong to the club, you don't get in, so nobody except club members knows for sure what lurks in those wilds now. The trees are too thick to see anything, even if you peek over the fence.

At one time there was a thriving buffalo herd. A flock of pheasants didn't last long. They knew what was good for them. They flew away. Other imports included black-tailed deer, mule deer, elk, red deer, bighorn sheep, moose, antelope, caribou, and Himalayan mountain goats. Shortly after the park opened, Corbin imported Russian boars. Some got out and, though rarely seen, their descendants still root around in the woods of Sullivan County and beyond.

The silliest question (for real!) ever asked by a tourist at a New Hampshire Visitor Center:

When does a deer turn into a moose?

Some of those escaped Russians may have partied with domestic pigs, in which case, the wild offspring would be feral pigs. The Russian boar can weigh up to 400 pounds. The feral pig can go 700, depending on the breed of its domestic mommy or daddy.

Boars are smart, which is why they're so good at hiding out. They can also be ugly if cornered.

If I were you, I'd avoid them.

Woodchuck

The woodchuck, also known as the groundhog, is not our most popular mammal. The woodchuck eats gardens. If they'd stay in the woods, meadows, or median strips where they belong, they wouldn't be so universally despised. But no. They have to sneak into our gardens and eat EVERYTHING.

Havahart traps work—sometimes. The problem is, what do you do with the chuck once you've caught it humanely? Ben, who lives on the Piscataqua River, made this observation: "Havaharts don't float."

In Durham, Phyllis walked for her health. She walked early in the morning and passed a lovely cottage owned by an older woman who was an avid gardener. Often she'd see the gardener at work in her fenced flower garden—pruning, weeding, mulching—to the heavenly sounds of opera music from an open window.

One morning, the opera music played softly, but the gardener was not in sight. Phyllis heard scuffling, heavy breathing, a profanity or two. She stopped at the garden gate. The gardener emerged from the bushes, disheveled, brandishing a bloody baseball bat, and shouting: "Those were my grandmother's goddamned peonies."

Fish

We fish and you can, too, if you purchase a license. Purchasing a license doesn't guarantee you'll catch anything, but it does guarantee you'll have fun trying. You can still-fish from a rowboat, troll from a motorboat, or simply stand on a bridge or beside a brook and cast your line. If you're brook fishing, be sure to sneak up real quiet. If they hear you coming, they'll know something's up.

According to the New Hampshire Fish and Game Department, these are just a few of the many varieties of freshwater fish we enjoy in our watery state:

At Lucas Pond the fishermen tell of a big trout named Leroy. He's been sighted. A few claim to have had him on the line, but Leroy always manages to escape. He's not only big, but also smart and tough. For proof of Leroy's existence, Jeff pointed to his aluminum boat. He said, "Leroy was barreling in close to shore after a school of kibbies. He lost track of where he was and smacked right into the side of my boat."

Sure enough, there was an indentation about a foot across and four inches deep at the nose. Just the shape of Leroy's head. "Did it hurt him?" I asked Jeff. "Well," he said, "it didn't do him any good."

Landlocked salmon, brown trout, rainbow trout, brook trout, lake trout, Sunapee trout (found only in Lake Sunapee—they're particular), largemouth bass, smallmouth bass, and pumpkinseed (pronounced *punkinseed*; usually they're little, as the name suggests; the biggest pumpkinseed ever caught weighed over twelve ounces; actually, two big guys share the record, one caught in Winnisquam in 1984 by Marcel LeBel; one caught in Winnipesaukee in 2005 by James Viar).

You will also find: black crappie, rock bass, white perch, yellow perch, pickerel, muskellunge, whitefish, shad, carp, cusk, and eel.

If you fish the salt water off the coast, you could end up with a mackerel on your line. Or a haddock. Or even a bluefin tuna.

Birds

New Hampshire has a lot of birds. Look up and you'll see them. Unless they're turkeys. Turkeys spend most of their time on the ground. Although they can fly, given sufficient motivation. Other popular birds include:

Loon

Known for its haunting and varied calls.

The Hairy Woodpecker

Known for its hair.

Partridge

Pronouced *pattidge* also called ruffed grouse. When alarmed, the adult will pretend to have a broken wing, stagger around drunkenly, and lead you away from the chicks. If you're walking through the woods and scare up a bunch of partridges, they'll take off with such loud fluttering, you'll jump, heart pounding, and say: "Damn pattidges." Well, you would if you were me.

Screech owl

This is another bird that'll get you going. A screech owl in the night sounds like somebody screaming bloody murder.

Crow

Open season on crows runs from August through November. And they know it. Seven crows will be sitting in trees yelling at you. Go in the house and come out with your .22. No crows. Crows all gone. They know the difference between a person going out to the mulch pile with potato peelings and the same person with a .22 and crow-shooting in mind. Crows know.

Bald eagle

Can have a wingspan of 7 feet. White head, white tail, brownish-black body. The bald eagle is our national bird, though Ben Franklin lobbied for the turkey.

23

Osprey

Almost as big as an eagle, but with a distinctive white underside. When an osprey is hunting, circling a pond for fish, sometimes they sneeze. I've heard it: *achoo, achoo*.

Turkey vulture

Sometimes mistaken for eagles or osprey because they're big and they fly. Up close they look like turkey vultures. Not pretty.

Cuisine

We like it simple. Meat and potatoes. We like our haddock stewed and our lobster mixed with mayonnaise and served in toasted hot dog buns. We like our corn fresh from the stalk, boiled, and buttered. We like tomatoes warm from the vine, especially those little cherry ones. We like our clams fried, our mussels steamed, our oysters raw and tasting of Great Bay. We also like our beans baked in a hole in the ground. This delicacy is called "bean hole beans." Only a few people, mostly Masons and Lions, know how to bake bean hole beans, and they guard the secret religiously. Through the summer, you'll see advertisements for Bean Hole Bashes, Bean Hole Bakes, Bean Hole Suppers, Bean Hole Blasts. Go. But don't ask for the recipe.

Being in our own way sophisticated and cosmopolitan, we also enjoy a variety of international dishes:

Canadian

Meat pie. Fried hamburg and ground pork, combined with mashed potato, onions, and various secret spices, including but not limited to cinnamon, ginger, allspice, and cloves. Baked between two pie shells.

Checklist

Here's a handy checklist with identifying characteristics for birds you might see in your travels around the state.

- **Canada goose**—Bigger than a duck, smaller than an ostrich, travels in flocks. Often seen in cornfields after the harvest. Listen for their distinctive call: "Good pecking, eh?"
- **Laughing gull**—Usually seen by the sea, but sometimes follows the rivers far inland. If a gull flies directly overhead, watch out for gull bombs. The gull's aim is deadly. After a direct hit, you'll hear the call: "Ha ha."
- **Black-capped chickadee**—Sweet little gray and black bird. Very friendly. "Chick-a-dee," he'll say. Which means: "Got any black oil sunflower seeds on you?"
- **Mourning dove**—Looks like a sad pigeon
- **Snowy owl**—White
- **Great horned owl**—Horny and somewhat egotistical
- **Scarlet tanager**—Red
- **Warbler**—(pronounced *waa-bla*) It warbles.
  But wait, which kind of warbler is warbling? It could be any of the following. Can you guess how to tell them apart?
  - Blue-winged warbler
  - Golden-winged warbler
  - Yellow warbler
  - Black-throated blue warbler
  - Black-throated green warbler
  - Cerulean warbler
  - Black and white warbler
  And my favorite:
  - Yellow-rumped warbler

25

Chilean

Chili. Fried hamburg combined with beans and chili powder, slow cooked in a Crock-Pot.

Chinese

Pie. Fried hamburg, mashed potato, and corn baked in a casserole dish.

English

Muffins. Toasted, then spread with peanut butter and jelly.

French

Toast. Bread soaked in eggs, milk, nutmeg, and cinnamon, then fried and slathered in real New Hampshire maple syrup.

Italian

Spaghetti. Noodles cooked soft, fried hamburg, onions, and tomato soup.

Mexican

Fritatoes. Corn chips with ketchup.

Russian

Dressing. Mix with chopped apples, onions, carrots, and cabbage, and you get New Hampshire coleslaw.

Spanish

Omelet. Eggs, chopped onion, and hot pepper mixed together and fried. Go easy on the hot pepper. Topped with ketchup.

Swedish

Meatballs. Hamburg fried in balls and soaked in pineapple juice.

Texan

Western sandwich. Eggs, onions, peppers, and ham between two slices of toast. Ketchup optional.

Schooling

How to fairly and adequately fund education has long been a mystery in New Hampshire. We just can't seem to work it out. For one thing, we don't know what *adequate* means. And the concept of fairness is elusive, too. The politicians and judges have been wrangling over these terms for years.

Right now most money for education comes through local property taxes. This is tough on account of the math. You can sit at your school district meeting, read the bottom line of the school budget, and figure out almost to the penny how much it'll take out of your pocket. So you say to yourself: "I like kids and think they ought to be educated, but can I afford $5,178.62 in property taxes on my shack by the side of the road? I guess I could cut back on . . . food."

This leads to testy discussions. We watch our pennies pretty close when it comes to town and school budgets. I had the illuminating experience of serving on the school board in my town for three years. I call it my three-year sentence. Went into the job thinking I was pretty smart, but found out real fast I didn't know anything, and couldn't do anything right. One eye-opener was presenting the school budget to the Budget Committee. The Budget Committee gets to siphon off all the fat before the budget goes to a vote at a school district meeting, where the townspeople can siphon off the rest of the fat, and anything else they see fit to remove. Right off, one of the Budget Committee members took me to task.

27

An engineer from the state came to one town meeting to explain the advantages of a filtration system for a proposed sewage lagoon. Since the engineer had specialized knowledge, the moderator told him to go ahead and enlighten the crowd even though he wasn't a resident.

The engineer set three glasses of water on the table. He held up the first one. It was brown. "After the effluent goes through the first filter," the engineer explained, "it'll look like this."

He held up the second glass. It was tan. "After it passes through the second filter, it'll look like this."

He held up the third. The water was clear. "After the third filter, the water is drinkable." And he took a swig to demonstrate. "Any questions?"

Fred raised his hand. "I have a question. How many filters," he asked, "does it take to turn a turd into a cookie?"

"I've already found a mistake in this budget," he said.

"What's the problem, Rusty?" I said.

"Right here on page three. Periodic tables. They're in the wrong place. They should be listed under furniture."

Politics

You tourists aren't likely to get involved in New Hampshire's "world of politics," but you still should know about things like how we fund our schools and run our towns and who those Free Stater folks are, just so you can understand us a bit more. Every little bit helps, because we're an odd bunch. Different, you might say.

Town meeting

Town matters are dealt with at our infamous town meetings, which are held in March. If you want to see a town meeting firsthand, that's perfectly fine. Sit in the back, be quiet, buy some Girl Scout cookies and a coffee, but don't even think about voting. Enjoy the show.

Here's how it works traditionally: Voters in each town assemble at the appointed hour. Each checks in with the Checkers of the Checklist, who check them off on the checklist.

The moderator calls the meeting to order, then proceeds to read all the warrant articles in order. Unless somebody moves that the reading of the full warrant be suspended, and that's seconded and the legislative body agrees: Aye.

Warrant articles are the items to be voted on. Usually there are 20 or 30 or more. The articles get on the warrant because the selectmen put them there, or by petition. If you can come up with a certain number of signatures, usually 25, you can put anything on the warrant.

After the moderator reads Article 1, he or she opens the floor for discussion, or questions, or both. The article gets discussed for a while until somebody says "Move the question." Then we move the question, unless somebody else objects. We can do a voice vote, yea or nay; a show of hands; or—and these are excruciating because they take so long—the dreaded paper ballot vote. Everybody gets in line, checks in once again with the Checkers of the Checklist, gets a ballot, marks yea or nay, puts the vote in the box. Then the votes have to be counted and the results revealed. You get 100 voters in the hall and have five or six ballot votes taking at least a half an hour each, there goes most of your day right there.

Why would anybody call for a ballot vote? (And anybody can.) They do it so their neighbors won't see how they're voting, that's why. If there's a new police cruiser up for a vote, you don't want the chief to see you voting "No." It might tick him off.

Oh, and another thing, articles can be amended. Say the article calls for $500 to dig the holes and put in the new sign at the transfer station. Somebody proposes to amend the article to

29

$250, saying that's plenty for hole digging. Then the legislative body must vote on whether or not to accept the amendment. If the amendment is accepted, that becomes the proposed amount. If it's not, you start again. Amendments can also be amended. If you want to get rid of a proposal altogether, amend to zero and that's the end of it. Or you can vote to table the article, which essentially kills it.

If you amend to zero, it's over. If you amend to $1, then the selectman, if they should have some extra money, could in theory transfer money to that line from somewhere else in the town budget. For example, if the Recreation Department budget is zero, the Recreation Department is not going to do much recreating. But, if the voters leave $1 on the line for the Recreation Department, the selectmen could move money during the fiscal year from, say, Building Maintenance, and Recreation's in business again. It's an old selectman's trick.

The myth of town meeting is that residents can argue and fight and call each other names, maybe take a swing or two, but once the meeting is over, everybody's friends again.

It's a nice idea, but not entirely true. Sometimes we get over it. And sometimes we don't.

My friend Tom Newkirk calls town meeting "the last blood sport," which pretty much sums up its appeal. In Northwood where I've resided the last 30 years (yup, they're just getting used to me), town meeting takes place in the Coe-Brown High School gym. A good many of us sit high on the bleachers looking down on the action—kind of like Romans in an arena. Oh, there's jousting and parrying, frontal assaults and sneak attacks, cheap shots and hits below the belt, hissing and cheering, thumbs up and down, and occasionally a pack of voles will run in, grab a Liberal by the Crocs, and drag her off. The bleeding is virtual, the passion palpable, and the spectacle well worth the price of admission. You don't have to be a resident to attend town meeting, but only residents can speak—unless they're given special permission by the moderator.

In a town I won't name on account of the high jinks, one of the citizens got on her high horse about videotaping town meeting. This was a few years back when setting up a camera to videotape was a good deal more complicated than pushing a button on your cell phone. The selectmen were against it because they knew what came next—that video-tape would come back to bite them in the butt. Sometime down the road, this citizen—

The most basic rule of town meeting is the inverse proportionality of time and money. That is, the more money is at stake, the less time the article takes to pass. The 1.7 million-dollar general operating budget passes in two minutes on a voice vote. The $200 to paint the cemetery fence takes an hour and a half.

whom we'll call Henrietta and who had a tendency to be irate—would say, "So and so said this or that at town meeting and I can prove it because I got it on videotape." The selectmen agreed this videotaping business set a bad precedent. This was, of course, before cable access television, which tapes and airs, in gruesome detail, everything from Zoning Board of Adjustment and Historical Society meetings to parades and talent shows.

But, way back when, Henrietta wrote some pointed letters to the editor, cited a few right-to-know laws, threatened to sue, and the selectmen caved. Town meeting day arrived and Henrietta hauled in her equipment. She set it up at the back of the hall. Unfortunately, although the video camera had worked perfectly at home, she couldn't seem to get it going at the

It's Official

State rock	Granite
State mineral	Beryl
State gem	Smoky quartz, aka, cairngorm
State tree	White birch
State animal	The white-tailed deer, aka, venison stew on the hoof
State bird	Purple finch
State shrub	Purple lilac
State wildflower	Pink ladyslipper
State fish	We have two. One for salt water, the striped bass. One for freshwater, the brook trout, aka, brookie or squaretail. Squaretails, especially the small ones, make real good eating, fried in corn meal with butter and garlic salt. Nothing better for breakfast. Except pie.
State vegetable	Don't have one. May I suggest eggplant?
State fruit	Pumpkin
Current celebrity	A tie between Tom Bergeron, host of TV's *Dancing With the Stars* and Fritz Wetherbee, who says "I'll tell you the story" just before he tells one each night on *New Hampshire Chronicle*. (Fantasy: Fritz partnered with Ludmilla Lightfoot on *Dancing with the Stars*. Wouldn't that be a kick?)
State syrup	Maple
State butterfly	The Karner Blue. It's an endangered species. Never saw one myself.
State insect	Ladybug
State soup	Pea

State pie	Canadian Meat. I'd give you the recipe, but then I'd have to kill you before you told my friend Pauline Dupuis, who'd kill me if she found out I'd given away her secret recipe. She really would. She'd chop me into little pieces with a cleaver.
State song	The oxymoronish "Old New Hampshire"
State amphibian	The spotted newt, endorsed by the *Manchester Union Leader*, our notoriously conservative newspaper, which described the newt as the "perfect symbol for ensuring ecology in New Hampshire . . ."
Ecology	Yup, we got it.
State nicknames	According to the New Hampshire Almanac: An Official New Hampshire Government Website, New Hampshire has four nicknames. Besides the familiar Granite State, the nicknames are "Mother of Rivers," "White Mountain State," and "Switzerland of America." This is all news to me. Then again, having lived here 54 years, I just call New Hampshire home.
State Motto	Live Free or Die, penned by General John Stark on the occasion of his divorce from his fourth wife, Natalie.

meeting. She fiddled and fiddled, plugged wires into different places, changed tapes, consulted allies. No luck. Wa'n't she ugly! But what could she do?

After the meeting, the moderator confessed to the first selectman that he understood Henrietta's right to tape town meeting, but he was kind of relieved when it didn't happen.

"That reminds me," the first selectman said, "I gotta put those fuses back."

33

First-in-the-nation primary

You might have heard, we've got a rich tradition in national politics as well.

Every four years, New Hampshire's secretary of state sets the date for our presidential primary. By law, it falls on the second Tuesday in March (traditionally Town Meeting Day), or "seven or more days before any similar election." In 2008, we held the primary on January 8. Had to. Pesky Michigan set their primary for the 15th. You count back seven days from the 15th, and there you have it, our earliest primary ever.

In 1976, a 28-year-old Democrat was elected by a Republican legislature to be secretary of state. Bill Gardner—who's been reelected every two years since—makes darned sure that first primary law gets enforced. He's also the man candidates must see in order to run in the New Hampshire race because he's in charge of the paperwork. From Lyndon LaRouche to Jimmy Carter, he's met them all. Among the unusual candidates: Austin Burton, aka Chief Burning Wood, who sent a four-foot snake skin to the state house in lieu of the $1,000 filing fee. And New Hampshire's own Jeff Costa, aka The Lobsterman, dressed as a lobster, complete with claws, skimpy wrestler tights, and a cape. Jeff founded the Crustacean Party. The fact is, just about anybody with $1,000 and a yen to run for president can walk into Gardner's office and walk out a presidential candidate with an official place on the ballot.

Facilities for travelers in need

Woods

If nature calls, there's always the woods. We've got lots. Be careful, though; that gravel road that seems to lead nowhere might be somebody's long driveway.

State rest areas

The state of New Hampshire maintains eleven rest areas year-round, and an additional five in warm weather. These rest areas are elegant. They include flush toilets, sinks with hot and cold running water, and most even have tourist information, guidebooks, and maps for your traveling pleasure. Some have vending machines. I-89 has three stops. I-93 has four. The rest are strategically positioned along heavily traveled non-interstate roads: Route 9 in Antrim, Route 3 in Colebrook, Route 4 in Epsom, Route 16 in North Conway, Route 25 in Rumney, and Route 2 in Shelburne—worth the trip for the birches alone; Shelburne is famous for its white birch forest. On the Everett Turnpike near Nashua (*turnpike* is a New England word for a highway that's been charging tolls since horse and buggy days), there's a Rest Area / Welcome Center.

Common Man restaurants

They serve good food, but they also feature New Hampshire humor in their restrooms. Take a seat and listen to Auntie Henrietta of Ashland tell stories. She's not actually there—it's a CD piped through speakers. She's some funny!

But she's not me. Every once in a while somebody will say: "Is that you I heard in the Common Man bathroom? Sounded like you." Compliment accepted.

Years ago the salmon used to run heavy up the Cockermouth River into Newfound Lake. Of course, when the salmon were running upriver to spawn, you couldn't fish for them. Wouldn't have been fair. They had their minds on other things.

Nancy was in the backyard hanging laundry when she heard shooting down by the river. In other parts of the country, like Boston, if you hear gunfire you head in the other direction. But in New Hampshire when you hear gunfire, you investigate. Which is what Nancy did. She walked crosscountry through the woods, clambered over a stone wall or two and came to the river, where she saw her neighbor Charlie sitting on the back with a .22 across his knees.

"Charlie, what are you doing?" she said.

"Shooting mushrats."

Nancy looked and beyond Charlie in the ferns she saw three beautiful big salmon, all laid out, not looking too lively. "Shooting mushrats, huh!" she said.

"Yup. Scaley buggers, ain't they."

You can find Common Men in Lincoln, Ashland, Concord, Merrimack, and Windham.

In a pinch

Find a McDonald's. Not public, but worth the price of admission.

Packing necessities

What you need to bring depends, of course, on the season. Clothes are good. Don't forget underwear and socks. Deck of cards. Travel Scrabble. A good book. (You've already got this one, so you're all set in that department.) We've got loads of stores, so if you forget something like Preparation H or Q-tips, you can buy them here. As for alcohol, the state-owned liquor stores in tax-free New Hampshire can supply all your needs from chardonnay to tequila at the cheapest prices around. People from Maine, Massachusetts, and Vermont regularly plan field trips to New Hampshire just to buy booze.

Cautionary tale: One time my family went camping and we forgot our sleeping bags. That was a serious oversight that caused considerable finger pointing and some heated words. Moral of the cautionary tale: Make a list. Check it twice.

In addition to the regular stuff like pants, shoes, and vodka, here are some essentials for New Hampshire travel, listed by season:

Winter

- Warm coat
- Warm sweater for under the coat
- Turtleneck for under the sweater
- Fleece vest for under the coat and over the sweater
- Warm boots with good treads. A pair of crampons wouldn't hurt. Even in metropolitan areas like Concord and Rochester, winter can get ahead of the maintenance crews. Crampons help on icy sidewalks as well as mountain trails.
- Warm socks for inside the warm boots
- Long underwear, top and bottom. You'll thank me later.
- Hat that pulls snug over your ears. Something furry with earflaps and a chinstrap works best. If you're planning to step into the woods during hunting season, fluorescent orange makes a good color choice, and it goes with everything.
- Mittens
- Gloves to go inside the mittens
- Lip balm. Just tuck it right in your pocket. You'll be glad you did.

Spring

* Deet

Summer

* Thong swimsuits for both men and women are de rigueur. (French for "the natives will get a kick out of them.")
* Sunscreen. That sun gets pretty intense last weekend of July, first week of August. You could get burned if you're not careful.

Fall

* A camera for taking pictures of the foliage. You'll want to take a lot of pictures. Come fall, our trees are well worth snapping.

Accommodations

Tourist accommodations run the gamut, from our grand hotels ($$$$$$$$$+) to chain motels ($$$ − $$) to charming country inns ($$$$ − $$) to practical but still-charming B&Bs ($$ − $) to slightly moldy but authentic hunting camps (¢). We've also got a spare room upstairs at my house if you're really in a pinch. It's a single bed that the cats think belongs to them. Unfortunately, the roosters next door start up about 4:00 AM, and we can't seem to keep the bats out, but it beats nothing. Why don't the cats catch the bats? I've wondered that myself.

You can also rent cabins by the lakes, timeshares with terrific views, or campsites to park your RV or tent.

With so many possibilities, you'd think you could just drive around and find a place to stay the night, but sometimes reservations are essential. During motorcycle weekend in Laconia, you'll be lucky to find a bed or a pile of hemlock bows on which to spread your sleeping bag within 50 miles of the festivities. Same for the Scottish Festival at Loon Mountain, the Blessing of the Bikes in Colebrook, or any time the New Hampshire International Speedway in Loudon hosts a NASCAR event.

The best spots in our 19 state park camping areas fill up pretty quickly, too. Summer is short, so most of the camping gets packed into a few prime weeks between the end of black-fly season and first frost. Although, some of the camping areas do open in February. Camping in New Hampshire in February? Why? To each his own, I guess.

You can reserve your mountain, woodland, lakeside, riverside, or seaside plot by calling 1-877-nhparks (1-877-647-2757).

Weather

Cold in winter, moderate in spring and fall, hot in summer—as a general rule. We have had snow in July, but it didn't stick. One New Year's Day, a couple years back, my husband and I took a spin in our convertible with the top down. It was about 60 degrees. That was weird.

Most years we get snow for Christmas, but not always. In the winter of 2007–08, most parts of New Hampshire got more than 115 inches of snow, not quite breaking the all-time record. Luckily, the snow didn't come all at once.

Meteorologists pretty much agree that New Hampshire weather varies. You can see 40 below with the wind blowing a gale in January, and 98 degrees in the shade with 90 percent humidity in August. Neither situation is particularly comfortable.

39

One of the selectmen, who may or may not have a drinking problem, showed up at the dump kind of unsteady on his feet. Maybe it was mouthwash that made his breath so tangy, or maybe he had one of those inner ear infections that upset your balance. Could have been. You hear different things.

Anyway, this selectman was heaving a kind of a heavy bag into the compactor. Kermit, the dumpmaster, calls it the crusher, because when a bunch of bags get piled up, he pulls the hydraulic lever from inside his little dumpmaster cottage and the steel slabs slam together. Everything gets squished, compacted.

This selectman was swinging this kind of a heavy bag like a pendulum, and when he worked up to the big swing to toss it, evidently he forgot to let go. He and the bag sailed over the railing.

Luckily, the crusher was pretty near full at the time so there was plenty to break his fall. There he lay, spread-eagled. His eyes were open but he didn't say anything. The bags puffed up around him. The customers gathered around, wondering what was the best way to snag that selectman out of there.

Pretty soon Kermit emerged from his little dumpmaster cottage looking owly. He walked up to the rail. Looked down in. Put his fists on his hips: "What the hell are you doing down there?" he said. "Get out of there. Selectmen don't belong in the crusher. They belong over in compost."

Then there are the perfect days. We have at least ten a year.

In winter, a perfect day is 34 degrees, bright sun and good snow cover for skiing, snowshoeing, or snowmobiling.

In spring, a perfect day is 60 degrees, bright sun, no bugs. Maybe the lilacs are blooming and the air is full of their scent. Perfect for hiking, shopping Market Square in Portsmouth, having a picnic, or bird-watching.

In summer, a perfect day is 75 to 85 degrees, bright sun, a light breeze. Great for grilling, miniature golf, fishing, boating, swimming, or snoozing in a hammock.

And in fall, the most perfect of perfect days, 65 to 70 degrees, bright sun, brisk breeze, color in the trees. Perfect for antiquing, fair-going, or hiking. Just take it in and say: This is the way life should be. Oh wait! That's Maine's motto. So just say: It doesn't get any better than this.

Occasionally, New Hampshire hosts hurricanes, blizzards, nor'easters, downpours, twisters, and microbursts. Sometimes there's flooding. But compared to the rest of the world, the weather here is fairly mild, much like the temperament of the natives.

Of course, most weather is fine if you're dressed for it.

2

Geography

New Hampshire—pronounced *New Hampsha* by most natives, *New Hampshirr* by television anchors, and *New Hampsheer* in Berlin by folks of French-Canadian heritage—is one of six states in the region called New England, which also includes Maine, Vermont, Massachusetts, Rhode Island, and Connecticut.

New Hampshire was named for a sturdy breed of pig, the black and white Hampshire swine; or for John Wallop, Lord of Hampshire and inventor of the paddle; or, more likely, for a town in the south of England. In some far, faraway places like Arkansas, people think New England itself is a state. It's not. Others believe New Hampshire is suburb of Boston. It's not. Yet.

The Connecticut River separates New Hampshire and Vermont along our western border. If you know what side of the river you're on, and what direction you're headed, you can deduce what state you're in. If you break the word Connecticut into syllables (sort of), like we did in fourth grade, light dawns over Marblehead: Connect-I-Cut. The Connecticut connects New Hampshire and Vermont and, at the same time, cuts a line between them.

The boundary between New Hampshire and Maine is less clear cut, running, as it does, along stone walls, streams, and from big tree to big tree out through the boondocks. Chatham

43

For many years the bridge that connects Springfield, Vermont, and Charlestown, New Hampshire, was a toll bridge. Gary remembered a crosscountry family trek that took a good three weeks. They drove all over—to holes like the Grand Canyon and peaks like Pike's. It was quite a journey in that old woody wagon with the three kids, including Gary, in the back. After all that time on the road, the family was relieved to be almost home. It was nighttime when they approached the toll bridge. Wouldn't it feel great to be in New Hampshire at last? Only one five-cent toll separated them from the Granite State.

But there was a holdup. Gary's dad stopped at the bridge behind a Cadillac with New York plates. The booth was lit up and they could see the collector rummaging around in drawers for a few minutes. Then he left the booth and walked across the road to the house—presumably his. They saw lights go on one after another, room to room, upstairs and down, as he passed through. Ten minutes later, he emerged. Walked back across the road to the booth, and handed something to the driver of the Cadillac with New York plates. The Cadillac moved on, and Gary's dad pulled up to the window. "What was that all about?" he asked the collector.

"Well," the old fella said, "that guy from New York handed me a hundred-dollar bill. Guess he didn't think I'd bother to make change."

has the distinction of being the only town in New Hampshire that you can't get to from New Hampshire. You have to go to Maine and double back. Well, you could try Hurricane Mountain Road—but I wouldn't recommend it.

At the tip-top of the state, we border Quebec, so naturally we're concerned about all those illegal aliens sneaking across the border on their snowmobiles and four-wheelers, mostly senior citizens, looking for cheap prescription drugs in Canada.

As you drive into New Hampshire from the north, you'll see that the WELCOME TO NEW HAMPSHIRE signs acknowledge our Canadian neighbors: "Welcome to New Hampshire. *Bienvenue.*" That means "eat your vegetables" in French.

At the rock bottom of the state, we border Massachusetts, but we try not to think about it. The signs at that border, near the state-run liquor stores within spitting distance of the highway, say: "Welcome to New Hampshire. Now go home. But first stock up on Jim Beam." Which is our warm way of saying: "You people drive way too fast and never yield. You frighten us. But we appreciate your business."

You can cross the state at its plumpest part from Charlestown to Portsmouth-by-the-Sea in about two and a half hours, depending on how fast you go and which roads you choose. Basically, New Hampshire has two big roads: Interstates 93 and 89 going up and down, south to north, and vice versa. You can make good time on those if you don't hit a moose. Believe me, you do not want to hit a moose.

The crisscross roads, east to west and vice versa, are not so fast—except for 101, but that's useless unless you're headed to Manchester from Portsmouth or vice versa. On 101 you're supposed to keep your headlights on at all times. That's because there are so many accidents—as if having your headlights on at noon will make a difference.

Me, I'd rather take the roads less traveled, though they can be tricky to negotiate. New Hampshire is not famous for road signs, especially on back roads, where, if you don't know where you're going, you'd best not go. And, most small towns along these roads have few if any streetlights. "Turn left just past the big red house on the corner where the big elm used to be" doesn't help in the dark.

You might think you're making considerable headway on one of these back roads and end up at a dead end. With so much water and so many hills, a lot of roads dead-end. We enjoy dead ends. Cuts down on traffic. If you start out on a tar road, and it turns to dirt, the dirt road narrows to ruts, and you sense a certain maliciousness in the trees closing in around you, you may be headed for a dead end. On the other hand, sometimes you get through the worst part, the road turns to tar again, and you're home free. Maybe when you puke out the other end, there'll be a sign saying WILMOT THIS WAY, ALEXANDRIA THAT WAY. But probably not. We don't bother much with signage. Just keep going. You'll end up somewhere. Eventually.

The trick is to be open to possibilities. Instead of having a specific destination in mind, just go. We call it, "Going for a ride." When you're just "going for a ride," it doesn't matter where you end up, unless, of course, it's Massachusetts. But you can't get lost. It's the New Hampshire way.

How long does it take to drive the full length of the state, straight up the middle, from Brookline to Pittsburg? Depends on how fast you go. But for most folks it's four or five hours, adding time for pit stops and turkeys. For some reason, some say global warming, the wild turkeys are proliferating. You'll see herds of them in fields and median strips, strutting and pecking. Sometimes they get it into their turkey brains to stand in the road. Thirty turkeys in the road, there's not much you can do, except wait for them to decide to move on. Which could take a while.

Indecision is a way of life for turkeys and voters in New Hampshire. Ask a New Hampshire voter his party affiliation, he may say: Republican, Democrat, Independent, or, more likely, None-of-your-damn-business. The truth is, most of us are fiercely Undecided. And we stay Undecided until we're in the booth, the curtain pulled behind us, pen in hand. It's the New Hampshire way.

Although there are official, defined regions of the state, which I'll get to in a few minutes, I have my own name for the southwestern/south-central part of the state: The Heart of Darkness. I have spent many harrowing evenings (usually in driving rain) careening down dark, lonely roads, late to a gig, in search of a library or historical society or a house with a light on. In my considerable experience, the online mapping services have no idea how to maneuver in The Heart of Darkness. My GPS forgets where it is, and, when

"If you go past the church, whatever you do, don't go over the narrow bridge," Winnifred said, after she'd given me an earful of directions to a storytelling gig. "But if you do go over the narrow bridge, whatever you do, don't take the dirt road to the right that goes out into the piney woods. But if you do take the road that goes off to the right into the piney woods, hang a U-turn as soon as possible. If you can't make a U-turn and find yourself about a mile out on that dirt road in the piney woods, be sure to honk your horn so they'll know not to shoot you."

I repeated that cautionary tale in another town to the south. A man in the audience corroborated. He said, "I know exactly where you mean. My brother-in-law was a selectman in that town and he told me all about it."

"Did your brother-in-law ever go over the narrow bridge, take the right onto a dirt road, and go a mile out into the piney woods?"

"No," the man said. "They would have shot him."

pressed, starts speaking Chinese. One night, headed home to Northwood from Keene, I ended up in Claremont. About ten o'clock I called my husband on the cell phone. "I'm in Claremont," I said. "I'll be home in an hour and a half."

"I thought your gig was in Keene," he said.

"It was," I said. "I'm taking the back way."

What I didn't say was: I don't know how I got here, but here I am, having driven for an hour and still no closer to home than I was in the first place. It's possible I was abducted by aliens, lost an hour, then dropped back to earth in the wrong place. Quite a lot of that goes on in New Hampshire.

In The Heart of Darkness, say, Unity, Acworth, Walpole, Gilsum, Bradford, North Sutton, East Lempster, Mount Vernon, New Boston, or Bennington, when the natives pull a sad face and say, "You can't get they-ah from he-ah," they're serious.

Which is not to say you shouldn't visit these towns. You'll feel as though the narrow, windy roads between stone walls have taken you back not just 20 miles but 200 years. Just when you think you're nowhere, a quintessential New England village pops up. Quaint? You betcha. They are 3-D Currier and Ives paintings with a hint of Norman Rockwell and a smidge of Grandma Moses—pristine town squares graced by classic white churches, a meetinghouse or town hall, a little park, and a country store where you can get pickles in a barrel, five varieties of whoopie pies, Megabucks tickets, and a carton of Winstons, cheap. You might even find, in warm weather, a couple of locals ready to engage you in banter like: "Hot enough for yuh?"

Or, "Cold enough for yuh?"

Or, if it should be raining:

You: "Do you think it'll ever stop raining?"

Local: "Always has before."

Or, maybe you can eavesdrop on a native conversation:

Local One: "How you doing, Lowell?"

Local Two: "Fair. Considering what I been through."

Local One: "What's that, Lowell?"

48

I see that YOU ARE NOW IN MASSACHUSETTS: GOTCHA sign, and panic sets in. If there's one place I don't want to go, it's Massachusetts. Particularly Boston. When I was a kid, once a year my parents would take my brother Robert and me Christmas shopping at Mammoth Mills Department Store in Manchester. (It's not there anymore—Mammoth Mills, I mean—so don't bother looking.) To get to Manchester from our home on Corn Hill Road, we'd take I-93 through Concord, heading south. Eventually, we'd come to that terrifying place where the highway split. To the left, the sign read BOSTON. I'll never forget the urgency in my mother's voice when she said to my father: "Turn right! If you don't, we'll end up in BOSTON!"

It was clear to me that if innocent New Hampshire folks like us ended up in Boston, by mistake or misfortune, we might never make it back home, or if we did, we'd never be the same.

"Boston!" Cousin Gob always says. "It's unnecessary."

Local Two: "Well, the last thing was a rotten set of stairs."

Main Streets in these villages are typically lined with colonial homes behind white picket fences or, even older, granite posts including iron rings for tying up your horse (pronounced *hoss*). In the town of Amherst, white clapboard (pronounced *clairbud*) houses and white picket fences are de rigueur, which means "don't even think about another color."

New Hampshire is diverse. Not racially, but we have other kinds of diversity—diversity of wealth (rich ones, middling ones, poor ones), diversity of education (PhDs, high school grads, school of hard knocks), political diversity (Republicans, Democrats, Libertarians). Used to be we were heavy on the Republican side, but lately, quite a few Democrats have sneaked across the border, and some old-time Republicans have gone to the dark side. A lot of us are died-in-the-all-natural-cotton

Libertarians. Plus we've had an influx of the ultra-Libertarian Free Staters.

We're diverse in opinion, but we get along. For the most part. Have to. Come winter we depend on each other to dig the cars out of snowbanks. Your car gets stuck in the snowbank crossways of the road in front of the house, the neighbors will come out to shovel and push even if you are a Liberal. It's the New Hampshire way. We are a tolerant people. We have a lot to put up with—including each other.

Different New Hampshires

As you travel around the state you'll find lots of different New Hampshires. For example, here's the difference between Durham (Seacoast) and Gorham (Great North Woods / White Mountains). In Durham, I was talking with high school students about a story by New Hampshire author Tom Williams called "Horned Pout Are Evil." Some of the students looked puzzled. "What's the problem?" I asked.

"What's a horned pout?" a kid said.

"What do you think it is?" I said.

"Is it a bird?"

A week later I was in Gorham working with third graders. We were writing a book about animals. "What kind of animals do you have around here?" I asked.

"Oh," they said, "we have foxes and deer and moose."

"Let's write a story about a moose," I said. "Now, to create a strong character, you must know what your character is like. What's a moose like?"

A boy in the back row raised his hand. I called on him.

"What's a moose like?" I said.

> In Claremont, a flatlander stopped a friendly-looking, rosy-cheeked fellow on the street.
> "Do you know where the opera house is?"
> "Nope."
> "Do you know where Washington Street is?"
> "Nope."
> "How about Tremont Square?"
> "Nope."
> "You don't know much, do you?"
> "Maybe not," he said. "But I ain't the one that's lost."

"Delicious!"

And that's the difference between Durham and Gorham.

Oh, and a horned pout is a fish.

Official state regions

New Hampshire is typically divided into eight regions, with some overlap.

Dartmouth-Sunapee

Gentle, rolling hills along the Connecticut river. Almost— dare I say it—Vermontesque. Think Dartmouth College, herb tea, and Birkenstocks.

But don't think too hard about those things, because the population in this part of New Hampshire is as diverse and per-verse as in any other. Philosophy professors live beside beaver trappers. Best-selling authors live beside Congregationalist ministers. Well diggers live beside brain surgeons. Free Staters live beside euphonium players.

Fun Fact: The rock band Aerosmith, which got started on the shores of Lake Sunapee in the 1960s and features New

Hampshire singer, Steve Tyler, is still performing, after more than 30 years and 11 platinum-plus albums.

Like Aerosmith, in the regard that they're still performing, are New Hampshire's folksinging twins, Rick and Ron Shaw, who recorded "I'd Like to Teach the World to Sing" with the Hillside Singers for Coca-Cola in 1971. It was a worldwide hit. Rick and Ron have performed together for more than 40 years. They've recorded a dozen albums. They also wrote and perform "New Hampshire Naturally," the unofficial state anthem.

Great North Woods

Rugged, rough, and remote. Lots of trees. More moose and bear than people. If you're seeking an outdoor experience, the Great North Woods has plenty to offer. And there's nothing in those woods that'll eat you. Except the blackflies. Between Mother's Day and Father's Day, watch out; the blackflies are as big as sparrows, and they'll swarm you. An old Avon Lady's tale is that Skin So Soft discourages them. Others swear by Ole Time Woodsman Fly Dope, which smells about like you'd expect. The only real protection is nets—head-to-toe bug nets.

Winter in the Great North Woods lasts from October until May, when the blackflies come out. Some years it snows nonstop. Some years, not so much. But cold. You betcha. It takes a hardy breed, a rare bird, to stick it out in the Great North Woods. If you've got hermit tendencies, this is the place for you. Lake Umbagog, almost entirely undeveloped, is more than 10 miles long, with 50 miles of shoreline, lots of eagles, loons, and osprey, all rare birds. At Umbagog, you don't watch the moose; the moose watch you.

The northernmost section of the sparsely populated North Country pokes into Canada. Here you'll find Colebrook,

Pittsburg, Stewartstown, Lake Francis, and the First, Second and Third Connecticut Lakes. It's bear country. Bring your tent and a sleeping bag, because you're aren't going to find much accommodation; maybe some cabins to rent or a hunting lodge.

Fun Fact: How do you pronounce the name of that big lake east of Errol? Some will say UMbagog. Some will say UmBAYgog. Either way, the natives will appreciate your asking. Umbagog is from the Abenaki, meaning "big fish here." Consensus in Randolph, when I took a poll of about 75 locals at a potluck supper, was an unequivocal UmBAYgog. Whatever. It's a big shallow lake, 15 feet deep on average. Warning to kayakers and canoeists on Umbagog: Watch where you're going or you'll end up in Maine.

Lakes Region

My guess is that people from away picture the Lakes Region when they picture New Hampshire. Island-dotted lakes. Cedar-shingled lakeside cottages. Elegant inns with blazing fires in stone fireplaces and Monopoly games set out for rainy days. Tennis on clay courts. Miniature golf and gopher bopping at Funorama.

In the middle of the state, a mecca for tourists, here the lakes congregate: Newfound, Winnisquam, Winnipesaukee, Squam, and Ossipee. Wolfeboro bills itself as the oldest summer resort in America. George and Martha Washington summered here. They were avid canoeists. And Martha, in particular, enjoyed fly fishing. Her fly of choice was the Woolly Bugger, which she tied herself.

These are big bodies of water, full of boats, fishermen, and swimmers in summer, beloved by generations of summer people who've bought up 90 percent of the shorelines and built

53

big-ass, I mean extravagant, seasonal homes. A few natives have hung on to the family homesteads, but, truth be told, the taxes on a cabin on the shore of Lake Winnipesaukee would make Bill Gates blink. These places are valued not by the acre but by the foot—one foot of waterfront on Golden Pond is worth more dollars than a story-teller makes in a year. We have a saying in New Hampshire: "If you have to ask what the taxes are on that lakefront mansion, you can't afford it."

A lot of rich and famous people, who'd rather I didn't reveal their names (Mitt Romney), own homes in the Lakes Region. Don't worry, they keep low profiles so you probably won't bump into any of them. But if you do, pretend you don't recognize them. That's the New Hampshire way. We respect other people's privacy. We mind our own damn business. And, anyway, we're not that impressed by fame and fortune. If you can change a tire in under five minutes, skin a muskrat, or bake good cream-o-tartar biscuits, then we're impressed.

Auntie lived on a back road off a back road off Deer Meadow Road in Carroll County. When the relatives came to visit, they noticed somebody building a house where there had been no house before on Deer Meadow. Curious, they hit the trip odometer to see how far the new people were from Auntie.

"You got a new house going in on the Meadow Road, Auntie," they said. "We measured and now you've got neighbors just six miles away."

"Yup," Auntie said. "They's a-crowding me."

Fun Fact: I mention Golden Pond. That's what New Hampshire playwright Ernest Thompson called Big Squam in the play that became the movie *On Golden Pond*, starring Henry Fonda, Katharine Hepburn, and Jane Fonda. Locals can point to the quiet coves where parts of the movie were filmed and the rock where Henry's boat got hung up.

My favorite movie set in the Lakes Region is *What About Bob* starring Bill Murray as a man with many phobias who seeks out his psychiatrist, Richard Dreyfuss, on vacation in the town of Winnipesaukee. There is no town called Winnipesaukee. And it wasn't filmed here. In the movie, the land's too flat; the trees too fat; the buildings too modern. Also, if Bill Murray were filming in New Hampshire, I would have heard about it. News travels fast in a small state.

Merrimack Valley

These are the towns and cities along the mighty Merrimack, which used to be one of the most polluted rivers in the country. Let's just say, no blackflies bred in the Merrimack, and those weren't pinecones you saw floating in the shallows. The fish grew big, but you ate them at your own risk. Now, though, the river's all cleaned up. People swim, canoe, kayak, and the fish are even bigger and thriving, as are the cities and towns— Franklin, Concord, Merrimack, Manchester, Nashua. The mills aren't mills anymore, but many of the buildings have been preserved and used as housing, offices, businesses, and arts centers.

Monadnock

These are the towns surrounding the most climbed and possibly most drawn, painted, and written about mountain in the universe. The MacDowell Colony in Peterborough has been a haven for artists for over a hundred years. They come. They draw, paint, write, compose symphonies, etc. MacDowell artists include James Baldwin, Leonard Bernstein, Willa Cather, Carolyn Chute, E. L. Doctorow, Louise Erdrich, and Eudora

Welty. And those were just the ones I'd heard of. There are hundreds of others.

A book, *Where the Mountain Stands Alone: Stories of Place in the Monadnock Region*, features over 50 essays and readings on how great the region is. It's pretty great. Woods, hills, brooks, and Quaint villages. That's Quaint with a capital Q.

This story has a ring of truth to it, but no guarantees. In Weare a farmer was looking for help on the back 40, cutting wood, clearing brush, etc. His neighbor recommended a young man named David, who needed some extra money as he was going away to college on a Rhodes Scholarship. The farmer took the young man on and put him to work.

A couple of weeks later the neighbor inquired as to how young David was working out as a farmhand.

"Well," the farmer said, "the boy's willing, and he may be smart, but he don't know nothing."

Young David—who wasn't much of a farmhand—went away to college, later became attorney general of the state of New Hampshire, and later still was appointed to the Supreme Court of the United States of America. Our own homegrown Weare lad, David Souter.

That's the story they tell in Weare about their most famous native son.

Seacoast

Thirteen miles of it jam-packed with attractions. You'd think you were on the Riviera, only not so warm, especially in February. From Seabrook to New Castle, it's big beaches like Hampton and little ones like Wallis Sands. Lots of rocks and starfish. Lots of places to spend the night or enjoy fried clams—the whole-belly clams, none of those spleeny clam strips.

Portsmouth, the metropolitan center of the Seacoast Region, has a lot to offer, including the highest number of poets per capita in the universe. They're everywhere—walking around downtown, perusing the boutiques, having a beer at the Brewery, sipping latte at Cafe Brioche, reading old books at the historic Atheneum, strolling through the colonial village of Strawbery Banke, or the lush gardens of harborside Prescott Park. Some of them are just sitting on park benches with far-away looks in their eyes. Sometimes you see them scribbling in their moleskines. A couple of these poets, in fact, wear berets.

TIP: If you want to see a pod of poets, try the Hoot at Cafe Espresso on the First Wednesday of the month, September through June, at 7:00 PM. This is not a subdued affair of five or six poets reading to one another. Often the Hoot attracts fifteen or twenty poets reading to a packed house. Portsmouth even has its own poet laureate, changed out every two years.

White Mountains

You'll find trails, hikers, ski resorts, skiers, snowmobile trails, snowmobilers, and out-of-breath bikers. It's bumpy. There are 48 mountains over 4,000 feet and more than 100 shorties (under 4,000 feet). There are many waterfalls, ponds that serve as reflecting pools for mountains, and multiple scenic vistas. My gosh, those snowcapped peaks—baldheaded in summer—will take your breath away. Mount Washington, affectionately known as The Rock Pile, is the highest mountain east of the Mississippi and north of the Carolinas at 6,288 feet, give or take. You can climb it, drive up it, or take a ride on the Cog Railway, first-class to the moon, pretty near.

3

History

One of the original 13 colonies, New Hampshire has a long and illustrious history. Before the Europeans sailed over in the 1600s, we had American Indians. Before that there were mastodons. Before mastodons, dinosaurs. Before dinosaurs we had rocks. We've always had rocks, except for when the rocks were molten and the ooze primordial. Later, a glacier or two slid through on the way from Canada to Florida. We know this because of our many glacial erratics (big rocks dropped by glaciers), as well as the drumlins and eskers, steep round hills and steep narrow valleys, respectively, carved out by the ice. My dad explained the whole thing when we rode the snowmobile to check the trapline in the swamp behind the house.

"That over there is a drumlin," he'd say. Drumlins were too steep to climb with our 1968 Polaris Charger, so we went around them.

"This hole we're plowing through is an esker," he'd say.

"Oh," I'd say.

New Hampshire history timeline

1000 BC   American Indians, including Penacooks, Sokokis, Ossipees, and Pequawkets, enjoyed hunting and fishing in our virgin forests and pristine waters. They gathered wild onions, berries, mushrooms,

The first Chinook

Some of the finest sled dogs running today are descended from one dog named Chinook. It's quite a tale. Arthur T. Walden went gung-ho for the Alaska Gold Rush in the 1890s, working as a dog puncher—not what it sounds like. He drove sled dog teams hauling freight. When Arthur gave up on the gold and returned home to Wonalancet, New Hampshire, he bred and trained his own teams, and eventually founded the New England sled dog club.

In 1917, a strange golden puppy popped up in a litter fathered by the son of one of Admiral Peary's Greenland sled dogs and a mixed-breed St. Bernard. The little guy, Chinook, was a "sport." He was distinct from his parents but distinctive in that his puppies all looked just like him. He was also a great, strong, big-hearted sled dog, who became the father of all Chinooks.

David Pagel's book, *The First Chinook*, tells the amazing story of Chinook's many feats—besides fathering all those puppies. He pulled the first sled up Mount Washington. He raced all over the state. And, at nearly twelve years old, he led a team on Admiral Byrd's expedition, a historic mush across Antarctica. It was during that mush that Chinook disappeared. He walked off into the snow on January 17, 1929, his twelfth birthday, and was never found.

Route 113A from Wonalancet to Tamworth is called "The Chinook Trail." If you look closely you'll see Chinook's picture on the road signs.

lemons, kumquats, and other comestibles. They avoided mountaintops. For one thing, there's nothing edible on top of a 4,000-footer except lichens, hardly worth the hike. For another, mountains were known to be the realm of the great spirits. The Great Spirit Passaconaway—The Wind Rider— drove a wagon pulled by wolves up and down the summit of Mount Washington, then called

Agiocochook. He and the wolves did not appreciate visitors. Now thousands of visitors ascend Agiocochook each year, forcing Passaconaway and his wolves to move to a condo in Waterville Valley.

898 BC   Pocacassawokeway sees a Bigfoot drinking from the Contoocook in Penacook (though both the river and the town were as yet unnamed). Nobody believed her.

1602–1621 Various European explorers and entrepreneurs pass through our state, noting trees, rocks, lakes, mountains, and more rocks. They don't stay long. Guess they couldn't handle February.

1602   King James I, obviously confused, names us Maine.

1623   Dover becomes our first permanent settlement, the settlers having learned that you can survive February if you eat enough chocolate, drink plenty of grog, keep the woodstove stoked, and play a lot of FARKLE. (See page 154)

1629   We are renamed New Hampshire, thank you very much.

1641   Massachusetts pulls a coup and takes us over. This is, indeed, a dark time in our history.

1673   Goody Cole of Hampton was arrested for witchcraft and found guilty of "familiarity with the devil." She had been seen turning into a dog, a cat, an eagle, and a black dwarf with a red cap. The only person ever convicted of witchcraft in New Hampshire, she got off a little easier than her counterparts to the south. She was lashed and served a short time in jail, but lived to the ripe old age of 88. Her ghost is often seen walking Hampton streets. According to Olive Tardiff in *They Paved the Way: A History of New Hampshire Women*, one police officer even had a conversation with her. He told her to be careful of the traffic. She told him she'd be fine, that she'd been walking these roads for hundreds of years. Which took the cop aback.

1679   Massachusetts cuts us loose, saying we're too high-maintenance.

1697   Hannah Dustin, kidnapped by Abenakis, scalps ten of them as they sleep on an island in the Merrimack and escapes. The Hannah Dustin Monument in Boscawen marks the bloody spot.

1719   First potato planted in the United States is planted in Derry. It grows and makes more potatoes, which are subsequently mashed with butter, salt and pepper, and declared "decent."

1720   First "Curves" opens in Derry.

1767   Wolfeboro becomes the first summer resort in the United States. Items available in Ye Olde Souvenir Shoppe there include magnets shaped like New Hampshire, moose key chains, and Old Man of the Mountain bobbleheads.

1774   New Hampshire becomes the first colony to declare independence from England. Others follow suit, eventually, but for a while we're hanging out there on our own, with King George III giving us the hairy eyeball.

1778   New Hampshire holds the first constitutional convention. Other colonies follow suit, eventually.

1788   We become the ninth state.

1789	George Washington swings by Portsmouth to say "Hey."
1808	Concord is declared the state capital and the question arises: Where are those 400 legislators going to park?
1811	Horace Greeley is born in Amherst. He founded the

1929. During the Depression, men cut wood for the town of Milan, so they could earn pay instead of getting handouts. Ozzie Wheeler was chopping out a stump along a road being built, working for the town to pay his taxes. Along comes an old-timer: "You know Oz, you should have been a doctor." Which got Ozzie kind of puffed up, until the old-timer added: "Because you sure can't chop stumps."

New York Tribune and was one of the founders of the Republican Party. Horace ran for president in 1872, but that didn't work out for him.

1823   The Belknap Mill in Laconia is built. It's now a museum, but the machines still run like clockwork and they still make socks, sold in the museum shop.

1830   Sarah Josepha Hale of Newport writes the epic poem "Mary Had a Little Lamb." Mary's sheep was a Hampshire ewe. When it was born it was called a new Hampshire ewe.

1853   Hillsboro's Franklin Pierce is sworn in as the 14th president of the United States. So far he's the only one from New Hampshire. What's up with that?

1859   Harriet Wilson published the first novel by an African-American woman, *Our Nig*. It took almost 150 years for Harriet to get credit for her

1952. The expression "What we goin' do then, Ev'rett?" or "What we goin' do now, Ev'rett?" originated with a road agent named Everett. When the town truck blew a gasket, the snowplow got stuck in the banking, the culvert plugged and flooded Hoss Head Road—whenever a tricky problem arose, the boys on the town crew would turn to Everett for suggestions. Occasionally, he had one.

"The big elm in front of town hall blew over and took out the statue of Franklin Pierce and three telephone poles. The sparks are flying, traffic's backed up in both directions. We can't get the backhoe through. We can't get anybody in or out. The chain saw's jammed and Mary Lou's in labor in the selectmen's office. What we goin' do now, Ev'rett?"

When the situation is dire, say, "What we goin' do now, Ev'rett?" It'll make you feel better.

           groundbreaking work, but, sure enough, she finally got her monument in Milford.

1879   Ebediah Baker sees four Bigfoots in an apple orchard in Lempster. Nobody believes him.

1884   The Great Migration of New Yorkers. Several dozen thousandaire socialites (they would be billionaires today), fed up with urban life and all that horse dung in the streets of the Big Apple, fled the city for what they hoped would be a northern Utopia. They drove their designer wagon train through upstate New York into Vermont where some became dairy farmers. The more adventurous pushed on into the mountains of New Hampshire, but after that first winter said, "To hell with this," and pushed on into Maine, where they finally found Shangri-la in the form of a spit they called Bar

Harbor because it had so many pubs. Some of their descendants still fish for lobster out of Northeast Harbor today. Others run B&Bs. I mention this only because you can still hear tinges of the New York twang in the "oi" that slip into some of the New Hamsphire accent, as in "Whoim I here? I'll tell you whoi. I'm here for a taste of those bread-and-butter pickles you promised me last fall. 'Bout toime, don't you think?"

1899   Governor Frank Rollins declares Old Home Week, exhorting those who'd heeded the call of Horace Greeley to "Go West, young man" to return for a visit at least. Many towns in New Hampshire still celebrate Old Home Day in August or September. Sometimes there are parades.

1905   Interested parties gathered in Portsmouth in 1905 to declare peace, ending the Russo-Japanese War, and enjoy a lobster dinner with vodka and saki, making New Hampshire the only state to host the signing of a treaty ending a foreign war.

1916   We hold our first presidential primary. The bumper sticker is invented. Henry Ford lost anyway.

1917   The first Chinook, the greatest of all sled dogs, is born in Wonalancet.

1929   The Great Depression bolsters the New Hampshire philosophy: "It'll go along like this for a while and then it'll get worse."

1938   The hurricane knocks down so many trees we don't know what to do with them, so we slide them into lakes and ponds for safekeeping. Some of them are still down there. You slide over a pond in

65

your kayak, look down. "What the heck is that?" It's a tree. In Grafton Pond in, you guessed it, Grafton, you slide on along, flatwater paddling, look down and see not only trees but stone walls. It's kind of creepy.

1952   We establish our position as the First-in-the-Nation Primary by law. That's right. By law our primary must be held at least seven days before anybody else's, causing one to wonder: What if another state passed the same law? What we goin' do then, Ev'rett?

1956   Grace Metalious publishes *Peyton Place*. Folks in her hometown of Gilmanton think some of the unsavory activities in this work of "fiction"—alcoholism, incest, affairs, murder, burying a body in the pigpen—sound kind of familiar. Folks in the rest of the state say: "Oh my!" Nobody admits to reading the book, but it becomes a best-seller.

1961   Betty and Barney Hill of Portsmouth are abducted by aliens for about two hours near the Indian Head in Lincoln. They didn't like it.

1961   Alan Shepard Jr. of Derry becomes the first American in space. He saw no aliens. Or if he did, he never mentioned it.

1963   New Hampshire institutes a state lottery, the first legal lottery in the U.S. in the twentieth century, giving Granite Staters the chance to "win a little, win a lot" or lose.

1973   Aristotle Onassis thinks it's a good idea to build an oil refinery in the delicate ecological system called the Great Bay estuary. Locals said no, no, no! No to

Onassis. No to Governor Meldrim Thompson, who thought the refinery was a peachy idea. No to William Loeb, the powerful editor of the biggest paper in the state, who thought an oil refinery in an estuary was a match made in heaven. Durham activists Dudley Dudley, Phyllis Bennett, and nearly a thousand others led the charge that resulted in a resounding No vote from residents, and led to the state legislature passing a bill supporting home rule. Ari and his refinery took a powder.

1973. The battle to save Great Bay was a long, tough one. Onassis, confident of success, commenced buying up great tracks of land. One farmer refused every offer. Money was no object to the Greek tycoon, so the offer for the little farm got larger and larger, far greater than any market value. Ridiculously huge. Still the farmer refused. "Why didn't you sell out, Albert?" his friends said. "Why didn't you take the millions and run?"

"Well," Albert said, "If I sold my house, where would I live?"

1975   Adam Sandler, five years old, moves to New Hampshire from Brooklyn, New York. Educated in the Manchester public school system, he grew up to be a famous actor, starring in many exceptionally fine movies like *Coneheads*, *Airheads*, and *I Now Pronounce You Chuck and Larry*.

1976   Bill Gardner is elected secretary of state and appointed guardian of our First-in-the-Nation Primary. He's still on the job, reelected by the legislature every two years, though he's never moved

any personal items—like photographs—into his
State House office, just in case he doesn't win the
next election. He's a true New Hampshirite. He
takes nothing for granite.

1977   The ladybug is named the official state insect, not
without controversy. In legislative committee, Mabel
Richardson of Randolph moved to "table" the motion
to honor the small, fast-moving insect, which would
have indefinitely postponed the proposal. Luckily—
and ladybugs are considered lucky—the motion to
table was shouted down. The Senate unanimously
approved the ladybug. And Governor Meldrim
Thompson signed the bill into law.

1987   Walter Bowers of Webster sees a Bigfoot in Bob's
Big Intervale next to Mill Brook in Salisbury.
Nobody believes him.

1988   Stonyfield Farm sets up its Yogurt Works in
Londonderry. Since then the little company has
grown and grown. Now it's the world's leading
organic yogurt maker, a Moo Hampshire success
story.

1989   Great Bay is designated Great Bay National
Estuarine Research Reserve, preserved by law.

1990   Bryar Motorsports Park opens in Loudon. On race
days, thousands of NASCAR fans pour in from all
over the country. The little cars with big engines go
around and around. You can hear them miles away.
Locals get headaches.

1994   Bossie is born. A Holstein with a white patch on her
shoulder that looks exactly like the Old Man of the
Mountain, her illlustrious career included serving as

Who's Who?

Match the famous person in New Hampshire history in column one to the famous accomplishment in column two

Column one

1) Fritzie Baer

2) Josiah Bartlett

3) Amy Beach

4) Mary Baker Eddy

5) Bode Miller

6) George Washington Morrison Nutt

7) Franklin Pierce

8) Augustus Saint-Gaudens

9) J. D. Salinger

10) David Souter

11) Celia Thaxter

12) Daniel Webster

Column two

a) First American woman to write a symphony.

b) Bested the devil and served in the U.S. Senate in the 1800s.

c) Signed the Declaration of Independence; hung out with the founding fathers.

d) Home-schooled native of Easton and World Cup skiing champion.

e) Supreme Court Justice, natty dresser, most eligible bachelor in Weare.

f) Best man at the marriage of Tom Thumb and Lavinia Warren in 1863, 29 inches tall.

g) Kept a garden on the Isles of Shoals, wrote poems and essays, hung out with John Greenleaf Whittier.

h) Fourth- or Fifth-worst president in U.S. history.

i) Sculpted Lincoln,the Boston Massacre, and the Double Eagle $20 gold piece.

j) Started the tradition of Motorcycle Weekend.

k) Founded the Christian Science Church.

l) Cornish recluse who wrote *A Perfect Day for Bananafish* and *The Catcher in the Rye*.

Key: 1j 2c 3a 4k 5d 6f 7h 8i 9l 10e 11g 12b

Butter molds are part of our farming history. Used to be everybody had a cow in the barn and a few chickens. During the Depression, this self-sufficiency served us well. Bartering was a way of life. You'd trade eggs for flour, tomatoes for potatoes, cordwood for pigs, etc. A lot of the bartering went on at the country store. One woman came into the store with a pound of butter. The butter was hand-churned, poured into the mold to harden, then turned out and cut into pound blocks. These molds had patterns on the bottom, so when the butter was turned out, it would have a little design pressed into the top.

"I'd like to trade this pound of butter," the woman told the storekeeper, "for a pound of butter." And she held out a good looking block of butter with a daisy imprinted on top.

"Why?" the storekeeper asked.

"Well," she said, "after I poured the butter into the mold, I noticed a dead mouse in the bottom of the churn. I screamed. The kids come running. And now they refuse to eat the butter. But I figured somebody else would eat it, because what you don't know won't hurt you."

The storekeeper thought a minute. "You wait here," he said. He took her pound of butter to the back room, smoothed out the daisy design and carved a little apple in its place.

"Here you go," he said to the woman, handing over the butter. "You're right. What you don't know won't hurt you."

spokescow for the White Mountain Animal League in Sugar Hill, which encourages spaying and neutering of pets. She was also the subject of a book called *Hey Bossie, You're a Spokescow!* by owner Mickey de Rham.

2002   Inventor Dean Kamen of Manchester unleashes the groundbreaking human transportation vehicle, the Segway, on a puzzled but fascinated public. This

energy-saving, user-friendly gyro-scooter has yet to
catch fire with consumers. President George W.
Bush, a buddy of Kamen's, took a ride on one of
the early models. He fell off.

2003   The Old Man of the Mountain falls and can't get
up, creating a hole in our hearts and a substantial
pile of historic rubble.

2003   The Free State Project selects New Hampshire as
the promised land for freedom-loving people. We
think it was our Live Free or Die motto that won
the day, because several other states, like Wyoming,
were under consideration. Organizers projected
that 20,000 Free Staters would relocate here by
2006. Doesn't seem like that many have made the
move. Then again, unless they're wearing I'M A FREE
STATER T-shirts, how would you recognize them?

2004   Exeter's Dan Brown's *The Da Vinci Code* gives *Harry
Potter* a run for its money as they vie for the top
spot on the best-seller list. Brown made so much
money the average per capita income for the state
went up 42 percent. A bill to fund New Hampshire
schools by creating an income tax just for Dan
Brown died in committee. "If we do that he'll
probably take his antigravity boots and move to
Maine," the chairman said.

2008   The Live Free or Die State becomes one of only
four in the country to recognize civil unions
between same-sex couples. Some people are surprised. Isn't New Hampshire supposed to be conservative? Aren't northern New Englanders kind of

71

old-fashioned? Yup. We are. And being conservative
and old-fashioned includes a long, proud tradition
of live and let live.

FYI: Senator Jack Barnes was among the dissenting voices on
the civil unions bill. He had this to say on the subject (quoted
from the *Concord Monitor*, April 8, 2007): "Baby Jesus could
come into my office and tell me to vote the other way and you
know what I'd do? I'd say, 'Baby Jesus, get the hell out of my
office!' Now, how does that explain it?" he said. "I'd tell Baby
Jesus to get the hell out of my way. I listen to this and to this."
(He pointed to his head and heart.) "Baby Jesus is not going to
tell me how to vote on that."

4

Speaking (and Understanding) the Language

The native New Hampshire accent combines the stretched out As of Massachusetts, the dropped Rs of Maine, and the hint of *oi* and *eew* from Vermont. We also have a tendency to drop Gs, especially at the ends of words. So, "We're going to Epping to do some shopping," sounds like, "We're goin' to Eppin' to do some shoppin'."

The accent varies region to region, but generally our cadence is swifter than the Maine drawl (gawd, those guys take a long time to tell a story!), and our enunciation less British than those Maaaasachusetts fellows with their Haaarvaaard gutterals. In Maine, they say "ayuh" and "wicked" a lot. We don't unless we're imitating Mainers.

We turn single-syllable words into doubles: dear is *dee-ah*, store is *sto-ah*, beer is *bee-ah*. As in: "Mildred, dee-ah, how 'bout you take the station waggin, slide down to the sto-ah, and get us a six-pack of bee-ah and some Fritos con chips for the pah-ty."

"Good idear, dee-ah. And while I'm at it, I'll get some ketchup and a can of pea beans for some of that Mexikin saltza."

A distinguishing characteristic of the New Hampshire accent is the "migrating R." It moves from one word to another. *Idear* picks up the R that *dee-ah* releases. For example, consider the sentence:

My aunt floured the board then rolled out the dough for crullers.

 My friend Sue grew up in Warner. She sells insurance and tries to lighten the accent for professional purposes. She said: "I can get that first R in War-nah, all right, but darned if I can say the second." I thought: There's two 'Rs' in Waa-nah?

Someone from away might say:

My ant floured the board, then rolled out the dough for cruelers.

We'd say:

My arent flou-ahed the bo-ahd, then rolled out the dough for crawlahs.

Note how the R in crullers moved into the middle of aunt. Note also, that the R in board disappeared, leaving two syllables instead of one.

Let's reverse the process. Here's something we'd say. Can you translate it into Away?

New Hampshire-speak: If you leave them bo-ahds in the do-ah yahd and it rains, they'll wahp and Arent Reeter will be pissed.

Translation: If you leave those boards in the door yard and it rains, they'll warp and Aunt Rita will be unhappy.

Remember Tina Turner? "Proud Mary Keeps on Rollin' "? Here we would say her name, Tiner Turnah. Again, you'll note the wandering R.

The fact is, most of us can pronounce Rs, but it hurts. I can pronounce whole sentences, whole paragraphs even, just like a network anchor if I concentrate. Or I can speak N'Hampsha just like my brother, my parents, grandparents, great-grandparents— all the way back through the generations. In other words, I'm bilingual.

In New Hampshire we like syllables and use a lot of them. **New Hampshire-speak:** Did Mahk get his dee-ah this yee-ah? Mahk did get his dee-ah this yee-ah, dee-ah. He bagged a two-hundred pounder with his thutty-ought-six oh-vah to Stanley Fo-ahd's fee-uld.

Translation: Did Mark get his deer this year?

Mark did get his deer this year, dear. He shot a two-hundred pounder with his thirty-ought-six over to Stanley Ford's field.

Unlike Mainers who drag out their words in a Down East drawl, we add syllables but say them fast, so our sentences clip right along.

This information is not intended to help you talk N'Hampsha. Fritz Wetherbee has put out a CD for that purpose. It's called *Speak N'Hampsha Like a Native*. It's helpful. Fritz, a seventh-generation native and television personality, knows his stuff. So go ahead and try the accent. Just know that many have tried before you, including famous actors like Michael Caine. (Truth be told, Michael Caine tried out a Maine accent in *Cider House Rules*, set in Maine, with sad results. And New Hampshire is even harder than Maine.) Usually imitators sound like they're from South Carolina, or a combination of

The lawnmower wouldn't start. The neighbor, who was handy with all things mechanical, had a suggestion: "Got any drag-ass?"

"Drag-ass?" Milly said. She'd retired to New Hampshire from away. This was her first summer in the mountains.

"Yuh. Go downstreet and get some drag-ass."

"Drag-ass?"

"Right. That mower's been sitting all winter. All it needs is a dose of drag-ass, and it'll be running like a charm."

"Drag-ass?"

"DRAG-ASS."

"Spell it," Milly said.

"D-R-Y-G-A-S. Drag-ass."

South Carolina and County Cork (pronounced *cock*). You kind of have to be born to it.

Our purpose here is to help you understand the New Hampshire accent, not speak it. Our purpose is to facilitate communication so you'll better enjoy your stay. And when your host says, "Would you please get the fox out of the draw," you won't be looking around for a pointy-nosed mammal with lush red fur. Your host wants you to fetch the forks from the silverware drawer. And, while you're right there, grab some spoons and knives, too.

Homonyms

These are words that sound the same to us. Say the first word the way you might regularly say it (if you're from California), and that's exactly how New Hampshirites say the second word or phrase.

ah: Are

ah: Our

This is pronounced like, "Open your mouth and say Ah." So the sentence, Ah, Nigel, how many of your folks are coming to our party? Really sounds like this: Ah, Nigel how many of your folks ah coming to ah pah-tee?

cock: cork

A rooster is a cock, you can cock the wine, or cock your firearm.

Variation: *Cockin' good* means excellent. As in:

"That Pinot Noir is cockin' good."

"What's it taste like?"

"Another."

coffin: coughing

During a potluck at the Bedford Women's Club, Josephine Fearon, a retired school counselor in her 90s, told a harrowing tale. Seems a couple years earlier Jo had arrived home from grocery shopping, unloaded the bags from the car, slipped on the cement floor of her garage and fallen hard. She'd broken her femur. She tried to crawl up the three steps to the door that led inside the house, but couldn't move. There she sat on that cold floor, her groceries scattered around her.

It was a chilly, rainy spring day and as she sat there, immobilized, the cold sank into her bones. The overhead door to the garage was open. She could see the street. She sat there for six hours. "Five cars went by," she said. "The drivers waved."

Finally, a garbage collector, driving by, noticed something wrong. He pulled over, walked into the garage, and rescued poor Josephine, who was nearing the end of her rope.

"I always wanted to be picked up by a handsome young man in uniform," Josephine told me cheerfully. "I guess I should have been more specific."

"You keep coffin like that you'll go into cardiac arrest and end up in a coffin."

con: corn

I grew up on Corn Hill Road so I'm always having to explain to people from away: Con Hill Road where ears of con grow on stalks. They used to grow a lot of con on Con Hill Road. Not so much anymore. It's all built up.

fox: forks

"Where the road fox I saw a mother fox and three babies. Wa'n't they cunnin?"

hoss piss: hospice

At town meeting the moderator says, "There's an article here to raise $500 for hospice."

The farmer says, "Got plenty of that soaked into my barn floor. I'm voting no."

khakis: car keys

I heard this on NHPR's Car Talk with Click and Clack. They were explaining the Massachusetts accent, but it's one of the few things that are the same here.

"Mother, I lost my khakis."

"Well, how do you expect to drive to work?"

"Not my car keys, Mother, my khakis. My tan pants."

"Why didn't you say so? They're in the wash."

shot: short

The new funeral director in town was surprised to hear the selectman was shot.

"Gosh, Peter," he said, "you'd think I'd be one of the first to hear about the selectman being shot, having to make preparations for the burial and all."

"I didn't say he was shot," Peter said. "I said he was *shot*. Not very tall."

You also take a shot with a gun, or drink a shot of whiskey. Best not to take a shot after you've had one, no matter what you've got a bead on or how tall you are.

snot: snort

As in, The snotty little snot was snotting up a storm because of his head cold.

airier: area

As in, "We may be lost be we're in the right general airier.

area: airier

As in, "If you open the windows the room will be less stuffy and feel area."

die-a-rear: diarrhea

As in, "I don't know what's worse, constipation or die-a-rear.

78

Vernacular

These are special words or sayings that might mean nothing, or something entirely different, in other parts of the country that aren't New Hampshire.

All set

A friend of mine from away said the first time a waitress asked her if she was "all set," she thought she was referring to the tableware. We say "all set" all the time. As a question, "All set?" means "Do you have everything you need?" As a response, "All set" means "I'm okay for the moment, but come back in ten minutes; I might need a refill on coffee."

Bring your pocketbook

Bring your pocketbook because this event or purchase is going to be expensive. "If you're planning to get anything to eat at the Sandwich Fair, you better bring your pocketbook. They want four dollars for fried dough."

Cellar

In some parts of the country, houses have basements. Here we have cellars. When the house is long gone, the cellar hole remains. Going out in the woods looking for cellar holes is an absorbing activity. If you poke around near the cellar holes, sometimes you can find the old dump. Dig around and unearth bottles, broken pottery, and so forth. Some of those bottles are worth money.

Cowt

If a local yells *cowt*, she means look out. "Cowt, Robit, there's a seagull overhead and she looks loaded for bear." Or,

"The driveway's like a skating rink. Cowt. You don't want to fall on your can."

Cunnin'

Cute, adorable, so sweet you could eat it with a spoon. Usually applied to babies or small animals, and their actions. "In kindygarten the kids were working with big plastic screws and nuts and gears, building plastic machines and so forth. Wally comes home one day. He says, 'Grammie, I'm the best screwer in my class!' Wa'n't that cunnin'?"

Clairbuds

The wood siding on a home, sometimes spelled, correctly, clapboards. We like to let our walls get used to the various coverings. Start with tar paper—let that age a year or two. Move on to Tyvek. Let that age a year or two. Then apply the clairbuds. Although, to keep taxes low, some people leave the tar paper or Tyvek up indefinitely.

"I've got to do some work on the outside of the house come spring. Mother's complaining about the drafts," Mo says.

"You gonna put up clairbuds?"

"No. Gonna patch the Tyvek."

Different

New Hampshirites use this word to express tolerance. We are a tolerant people. We have to be. We have a lot to put up with. Sometimes we say *different* because we have no firm opinion one way or another. We're open to suggestion. Or if we do have an inkling of an opinion, we believe it best to withhold comment.

"Grammie, what do you think of Maxine's new boyfriend?"

"He's different."

"How's the beans? I cooked them in maple syrup instead of molasses. Do you think they're too sweet?"

"They're different."

"So your daughter, her three boys, and the incontinent rottweiler are living in your cellar. How's that working out?"

"It's different."

Royal told his friend Urban: "It was a nippy day but the sun was out. I happened to scrape the frost off the window, and looked across the road to Ezra's place. There he was all laid out on his porch in his skivvies, getting a tan. Cold don't bother, Ezra."

Urban said, "Geez, Royal. Ezra all laid out on his porch that cold day in his skivvies. Must have been quite a sight."

Royal said, "Wa'n't pretty."

Dinner

The noontime meal. Going out to dinner, which we don't do very often, might involve meeting a friend at the Weathervane at 11:30 AM for a bowl of chowder or a clam boat. The evening meal is called *supper*. If it's held at a church and you pay $7.50 for ham and beans, it's called a Church Supper. A Potluck Supper is where everybody brings a dish and you hope they don't all involve tuna and noodles.

Frappe

I don't know what they call these in other parts of the country, but here a frappe is milk, syrup and ice cream beaten together. A milk shake, on the other hand, is milk and syrup, no ice cream.

Gomin

Impressively big. As in, "That center on the basketball team is gomin, and so's her sister Ruthie." It can also imply clumsy, as in "He was a great, gomin fella. Squeezed through the door,

81

tripped over the cat, fell the full flight of stairs to the cellar and landed in a heap on the cement floor."

"Did he get hurt?"

"Didn't do him any good."

Hoss

An animal for riding. As in, "On the old television program *Bonanza*, Hoss Cartwright liked to ride his hoss around the ranch."

House room

Worthless. As in the expression "I wouldn't give it house room."

Jimmies

Chocolate candies you sprinkle on ice cream. If the girl at the ice cream counter says, "Do you want jimmies?", do not reply "No, I want my own."

Loaded for bear

A hunting term. If you put the heavy charge into the muzzle-loader, you're loaded with enough firepower to shoot a bear. If you're out partridge hunting, you use the light load. When a person is on a mission or a rampage, he's loaded for bear, prepared for big game. When a seagull is loaded for bear, the bird looks full and ready to let a big one drop.

Pissa

Something of high quality, as in, "That blue Corvair is a real pissa." It can also mean the opposite.

Harold wore his new fedora to his grandfather's house, where the two spent a rainy afternoon chatting and playing cards. Gramps never mentioned the hat, though.

As Harold got up to leave, he said, "How do you like my new hat, Gramps?"

Gramps thought a minute, then said, "It's a pissa."

There's more to the expression, I'm told. The whole thing goes like this, in the case of the hat: "I hope that hat is waterproof, because it's a real pissa."

Poim

A one-syllable word that means poem. A poit writes poitry. Robert Frost wrote a poim called "New Hampshire." He lived for a time at the Frost Place in Franconia, not to be confused with the Frost House on the campus of Plymouth State University (previously Plymouth State College, previously Plymouth Teachers College, previously Plymouth Normal School), where he lived from 1911–12. Also not to be confused with the Frost Farm in Derry where he lived from 1910–11.

Right out straight

Nothing to do with sexual orientation. It means "too busy." You're moving so fast you create your own breeze and your hair gets blown right out straight behind you.

Since Christ wore knickers

The practice in question has been going on for a long, long time, since Fennimore Christ—who lived in the 1800s and was known for dressing nattily—was young enough to wear knickers.

Spleeny

Weak, unworthy. "Those goddamn Red Sox would have won that last game if they weren't so spleeny."

Stickler

Pronounced *stick-lah*. A stick-lah won't give. A stick-lah sticks to the exact rules. A stick-lah can make your life miserable, for example, if you want to dump your dump at the dump and your dump sticker is expired. If the dumpmaster is a stick-lah, he'll turn you away and grin while he's doing it.

In these small towns we have a high percentage of stick-lahs stickling it to their neighbors. Why? Because they can. And for some reason, they seem to think they should.

Ugly

Nothing to do with one's appearance, but rather with one's temperament. *Ugly* means mean, ornery, grouchy, testy.

Cub the plumber showed up at Mo's house with his toolbox. The toilet wasn't flushing just right, and Mo thought it was time he called in an expert. "The bathroom's the first door on the left," Mo told Cub. "Go right in, but pull the door tight shut behind you. Mother's taking a tub, and if there's a draft, she'll be ugly."

Of course, an ugly person can still be ugly in the traditional sense, as well.

Visit

Can mean to physically move yourself to somebody else's house to spend social time with them, but more often it means to talk. "Sophie's quite a talker. She likes to visit."

Wa'n't

Pronounced *want*. It's short (pronounced *shot*) for "was not" or "were not." As in "The coleslaw wa'n't bad, and the beans wa'n't nothin' to sneeze at, but the brown bread was out-standin'."

Yogut

Made from milk and sometimes flavored; if you eat too much yogut, yo gut might grow. Our own Stonyfield Yogurt company started with a cow and a pail and is now bullish in the the dairy field.

New Hampshire place names

Nothing lets people know you're from away quicker than mispronouncing the name of a place. Here are a few common mispronunciations alongside the correct pronunciation.

	wrong	**right**
Alstead	All-stead	Al-stead

There's no All in Alstead.

Berlin	Ber-LIN	BURR-lin

As in, "Burr, it's cold in Berlin come February." BURR-lin, New Hampshire, is pronounced the opposite of Ber-LIN, Germany.

Boscawen	Bos-COW-in	Bos-quine, Bos-quin
		Bos-ka-wen, Bos-coin

Even the people who live there debate the pronunciation.

Chatham	Chat-em	Chat-ham

Chat-em's in Massachusetts. We prefer ham with our Chat. Chatham is also known as the Sister City to Stow, Maine.

	wrong	**right**
Chicorua	Chick-o-RUE-a	Chick-OR-rue-ah

Bald, pointy peak in the town of the same name.

Coos	Coos	Co-OS

A dove coos. The county is Co-OS.

Contoocook	CON-too-cook	Con-TOO-kuk

As in, "You can't cook."

"Can too cook."

Also known as Tooky.

Manchester	Man-ches-ter	Manch-vegas

Milan	Mi-LAAN	MY-lan

As in the folk song, "This lan is your lan, this lan is My-lan."
In Milan the saying goes: "Milan's dumb, but the next town's
Dummer."

Plaistow	Plass-TAU	Plass-TOE

The native said, "It's Plass-toe like in toe, not Plass-tau like in cow."
Her friend said, "I say Plass-tau like in cow."
The native said, "That's because you've only lived here twenty-five
years."

Piscataqua	Piss-ka-TAU-qua	Piss-KAT-a-qua

Piscataqua does not rhyme with Chautauqua. It's the big river that
separates Maine and New Hampshire, and it's got a KAT in the middle of it.

Westmoreland	West-MORE-land	WES-ma-lin

The faster you say WES-ma-lin, the more you'll sound like a native.

5

Natives

A friend of mine tells of the time he and a couple
of buddies from Portsmouth, as yuppified a tourist mecca as
you'll find in New Hampshire (and I mean that as a compliment), were breakfasting in a diner in a North Country town,
possibly Colebrook, as un-yuppified a town as you'll find in
New Hampshire (also a compliment). They were dressed for
fishing—in flannel, denim, and Bean boots. Maybe one had a
vest dotted with dry flies, mooselook warblers, and gummy
worms. Maybe another sported his summer growth of beard
and a pair of Gore-Tex overalls, and the third had his long white
hair pulled back in a ponytail under a well-worn NRA cap.

A family of tourists slid into the diner, and the father, upon
noticing the three fishermen hunched over their sausage, hash
browns, toast, and eggs, stage-whispered to his clan: "Look!
Natives!"

'Course, they weren't natives at all. The lawyer, architect,
and oncologist were Ivy League–educated transplants. Which
just goes to show, you can't judge a native by his overalls and
mooselook warblers.

In New Hampshire we are inordinately proud of our native
status. If you've lived in New Hampshire all your life (so far),
that's considered an accomplishment. The wide world beyond
our borders beckons; it takes considerable self-control to resist

Cub the plumber walked into one of those fancy houses on High Street. The owners had gone on vacation, and while they were gone, their furnace broke and their pipes froze. They came back to a big mess. They called Cub right away. In the hallway, Cub stopped and listened. He could hear water dripping. He looked up. Directly overhead was one of those big globe lights, spilling over with water. One of the pipes in the upstairs bathroom must have split.

"Funny place for a fishbowl," Cub said.

That's what I call dry humor.

the lure of exotic places like Fryeburg over to Maine.

If you've lived in the same town in New Hampshire all your life (so far), that's an even greater accomplishment. Your roots run deep, you're related to half the townsfolk, and you're probably working in the family business—hardware, farming, carpentry, roads, paper mill. (Although, sadly, nearly all the mills have gone.)

If your parents and grandparents on both sides were born here, bonus! This shows commitment. Go ahead, call yourself a native. But don't say it too loud. The hard-core definition of *native* in the state of New Hampshire is "Five generations in the ground."

Some people become honorary natives because of their attitudes. At a meeting of the Walpole Society for Bringing to Justice Horse Thieves and Pilferers of Hen Roosts and Clotheslines, a man told how he and three others in the Society had formed a subcommittee. They called themselves the OFC, short for Old Farts Club. During town cleanup day, the four Old Farts, all retirees and transplants from more-populated places, were picking up trash beside one of the main arteries. A lost stranger pulled up beside them, slid his window down, and asked: "Do any of you know how to get to Hancock?"

There was a long pause. Then the four Old Farts answered as one: "Yup."

That's New Hampshire attitude. Enough of that and, in my book at least, you'll qualify as an honorary New Hampshirite, whether or not you're a native. To recap and distinguish:

Native is an accident of birth.

To be a New Hampshirite is a way of being.

Got it?

Real natives

Example 1

Clarence listened to his neighbor go on and on about the efficiency of her new woodstove. "You should get one, Clarence," Aggie said. "You'll use half the wood you used to."

"Maybe I'll get me two," Clarence said. "Then I won't need any wood a'tall."

Example 2

At the meat-packing plant, Marcel tried to free up a stalled conveyer belt with a broom handle. The belt started to move, caught the broom, snapped it, and one of the pieces hit Marcel in the forehead, knocking him to the floor, where the boss, a New Hampshirite through and through, found him some time later.

This sign was not painted by a native:

WICKED GOOD LATTES AHEAD

This sign probably was:

BARBECUED CHICKEN, BEEF & DOGS

"Marcel, what happened?" the boss said.

Marcel explained. The boss listened, frowning. He picked up the two pieces of the broom. "Marcel," he said, "you broke our good broom!"

Example 3

George was out in the door yard working on a tractor from his tractor collection. His neighbor, Gilbert, an old-time farmer and native (five generations in the ground), came by. "You got a good heavy chain, George?"

The antiques dealer paid a fair price for the pressed-back oak rocker. "That belonged to my grandmother," the seller said. "Sentimental value?" the dealer said.

"Some. And would you park in the back and take the chair out through the back door? She's in the front bedroom upstairs, and she might get upset if she sees it going."

"In the barn," George said.

"Could I borrow it?"

Gilbert was a good neighbor. He didn't ask for much. George had to stop work on the tractor and rummage around in the barn for fifteen minutes, but he finally came up with a good, strong hauling chain.

Gilbert thanked him.

"I'm surprised you don't have a chain over to the farm," George said.

"I've got a chain," Gilbert said. "I just didn't want to break mine."

Example 4

Over in Hebron during the days of party lines, Hattie had a reputation for listening in on other people's conversations. One day when a couple of her neighbors were discussing something kind of private, they happened to think, Maybe Hattie's listening in. So one of them yelled into the phone: "HATTIE, HANG UP THE PHONE!"

Hattie yelled back, "I AIN'T LISTENING. I'M CLEAR OVER BY THE SINK."

Fran asked Lois if she'd be at their neighbor's funeral on Saturday. "No," Lois said, "I ain't going." "Why not?" Fran said. "Why should I? She wouldn't go to mine."

Example 5

Linwood Rogers used to sell picnic tables for 16 dollars each. This was years back when picnic tables were less expensive than now. This fella pulls up in a pickup. "How long does it take you to make one of those picnic tables, Linwood?" he asks.

"About four hours," Linwood said.

"Four hours, sixteen dollars," the fella said, doing some quick calculations. "That's about four dollars an hour, isn't it?"

"Yup," Linwood said.

The fella said, "Could you make me a picnic table for three dollars an hour?"

"Sure," Linwood said, "but it'll take a little longer."

Native organizations

The Walpole Society for Bringing to Justice Horse Thieves and Pilferers of Hen Roosts and Clotheslines is the last organization of its kind in New Hampshire. In the 1800s, Charlestown, Keene, Marlborough and Nashua boasted similar clubs, but they petered out. Since 1821 the W.S.F.B.T.J.H.T.A.P.O.H.R.A.C. has been doing what it does best, i.e., not much. And they've got 183 years' worth of minutes to prove it.

Though no thief has ever been caught by these vigilantes, a few horses were reclaimed. One in 1841. Another in 1874 (dead, unfortunately). In 1928 the Society spent $28.44 (mileage? meals?) to chase Harmon Watkins's horse clear to Massachusetts. When the horse was returned, even Harmon agreed it wasn't worth that kind of money.

This costly episode was, in fact, the last "professional endeavor" undertaken by the W.S.F.B.T.J.H.T.A.P.O.H.R.A.C. Nevertheless, the Society canters on. Current membership: 240, despite the dearth of horses, hen roosts, and clotheslines in Walpole.

The Horse Thieves, as they're known around town, nowadays don't do much except put on a banquet every other year, with a featured speaker like filmmaker Ken Burns (*The Civil War, Baseball, Jazz,*) who lives in Walpole. The first time Burns was scheduled to speak, he got laryngitis. Reporters showed up at the scheduled hour. No Ken Burns, but one of the members pinch-hit with a rendition of the Society's colorful history. Some of the remarks made the wire services, and before you knew it, a man in California had heard about the Horse Thieves and wanted to join.

He couldn't.

You must be an adult male resident of Walpole to enjoy the rights and privileges of the W.S.F.B.T.J.H.T.A.P.O.H.R.A.C. Among these rights and privileges—your name printed on a poster. Originally the posters had a practical application: Only Society members received its protection. If you weren't a member and your horse got stolen, or your clothesline or hen roost got pilfered, tough luck. Basically, the poster alerted thiefs as to whose horses were up for grabs, and whose weren't.

Dues started out at $1 per year, rose to $3, then fell back to $2. Yup, two dollars and your signature in the membership book buys a lifetime membership—so long as you don't move out of Walpole. A couple of times it turned out a recruit lived just over the line in Alstead or Westmoreland, or in later

How to execute a New Hampshire hug

Step one: Stand shoulder to shoulder with the potential huggee, facing forward.

Step two: Fold your arms tight across your chest.

Step three: Turn just your head to face the potential huggee as the potential huggee does the same.

Step four: Nod.

years moved to a retirement facility in another town. These situations created problems. Big problems.

I asked a longtime officer whether they'd ever had any trouble with ladies wanting to join.

"Yup," he said.

Hermits

Occasionally, natives go native. I speak of the rare and respected New Hampshire hermit. Used to be just about every town had one somewhere in the back woods—not so much now. Not as much back woods as there used to be. A doctor told me how he accompanied his father, also a doctor, on a house call for a hermit. Old Nate hadn't been seen in some time. He kept to himself in his cabin on the side of Ragged Mountain, but walked to town occasionally for supplies. Nobody'd seen him in a while, and the folks who kept track of such things were concerned. Maybe the doc would take a walk out to Nate's place to see if he was ailing.

The son, just a boy at the time, went along. After a two-hour hike, medical bag in hand, Doc and son arrived at Nate's place. They called out to him. No answer. Tried the door. Locked from the inside. Uh-oh.

Out on Highland Lake in East Andover, some visitors were trying their luck fishing. They sat in their boat catching nothing, while no more than 100 feet away an old fella was hauling them in one after another. The visitors tried worms and salmon eggs. They cast dry flies and wet. They pulled out every lure in their tackle boxes. No luck. Not even a nibble.

Finally, in frustration, one called out to the old fella: "How come you're catching fish, and we're not?"

The old fella replied: "I'm a native."

There was just the one window, high up, open a crack. Doc hoisted his son up on his shoulders and instructed him to squeeze through that window. Which the boy did. He squeezed through and fell to the floor in the cabin. When he raised his head, there was Nate, in his Morris chair, with a shotgun cocked and pointed in the boy's direction.

Once the boy explained that he'd come with his father to help, Nate said, "Go ahead, then. Open the door and let the doc in."

Nate, it seemed, felt so poorly, he'd hunkered down to die. He told Doc his symptoms. Doc didn't think he was dying at all. He diagnosed acute constipation and administered an enema.

When the deed was done, Nate asked Doc how much he owed him for the house call.

"Well," Doc said, "the boy and I will have spent the good part of a day hiking out here, fixing what ails you, and hiking back. I guess five dollars will cover it."

Nate handed Doc a ten. "That first one felt so good, Doc," he said, "I'll have another."

Friendly New Hampshire

There's a myth that New Hampshire people are cool, remote, even unfriendly. This is not so. Some say we are slow to warm up to people. It's true, we're not apt to jump directly from how-do-you-do to come-on-over-for-pot-roast-Saturday-night. Generally, we reserve pot roast (and Saturday nights) for family.

Neighbors? We get acquainted eventually. No big rush.

 In New Hampshire, we adhere to the tradition of minding our own business. Go ahead—spend all your money on lottery tickets, put a Jacuzzi in your backyard, join a coven, adopt a shih tzu, grow a couple marijuana plants among the tomatoes, put a stud through your nipple, marry a lawyer—just don't make a big deal about it, and we'll leave you be. None of our business.

Of course, we also like to keep track. A friend of mine stopped by the coffee shop in town. She bought a cup to go and mentioned to Sue, the coffee maker, that she was on her way to visit someone just down the road. "Oh, who?"

"Becky Rule," my friend said. "And I'll take a coffee for her, too."

"Don't bother," Sue said. "She doesn't drink coffee."

We try to mind our own business, but sometimes we weaken. Especially in times of trouble. Or potential trouble.

In Woodford, during party line days, the road agent's wife got a call in the middle of the night. Big snowstorm and, wouldn't you know, the plow truck got stuck. "Go down to the barn, Sally, start up the tractor and bring her down the hill to pull me out," the road agent said.

Sally said "Okay, soon's I get my boots on."

Then another voice piped up on the line, a concerned neighbor: "Sally, don't you dare go out in this weather. You stay to home and let the men sort it out."

A tourist standing at the top of Mount Major looked down upon Lake Winnipesaukee and was more than a little impressed by the beautiful lake. "That is one huge body of water," he said to a native. "Yup," the native replied. "And that's just the top of it."

If you're going to move in and move out within the decade, no sense getting attached. Our next door neighbors had lived in the little house a year or two before we got acquainted. But one day, sure enough, a moose appeared in the road. And loitered. The neighbors stood in their yard, watching the moose. We stood in ours. Eventually, the moose struck out across the swamp and disappeared. I initiated a conversation. It went something like this: "Nice moose."

"Yup."

Good fences make good neighbors, Robert Frost wrote, sarcastically—then again, he was born in California. New Hampshire people do believe good fences make good neighbors. Get too friendly with your neighbors, first thing you know they're buggin' ya. Go careful when it comes to neighbors; they know where you live.

How to recognize a native New Hampshirite

Habitat

We can be found at the local gas station, the general store, yard sales, the gun and ammo shop, Sam's Club. Or at the dump, picking. Rule of thumb for dump picking: Try not to bring home any more than you deposited.

You can also find us in the woods, hunting, getting wood, maybe walking our property lines to check for infringements. We like the woods, but need a practical reason to go out into them. We don't hike, for example. No point to it.

You can find us on the water in a boat, fishing. We do not throw the fish back unless they're too small or bony. We eat them. On a real hot day, you might catch one of us taking a dip, but that would be a rare thing since most of us don't own bathing suits. You will never find a New Hampshire native water-skiing. Getting dragged around behind a boat on a string? What's the sense of that?

We will not be found at a movie theater, a mall, or a fitness club. Why pay $8 to go to a movie when you can rent it a month later for 99 cents? And Hollywood hasn't made a good movie since Cary Grant died, anyhow. Malls are, like Boston, unnecessary. You can't buy bar and chain oil at a mall. Or groceries. Or a pound of spikes. Or 50 pounds of goat feed. Or a house jack. There's nothing at a mall a person needs. As for a fitness club, why would anybody pay money to tug on pulleys or trot on a conveyer belt when they could do real work?

Fashion

Men and women dress pretty much the same, except men wear more hats. In summer, it's billed caps, with a variety of embellishments from the familiar B of the goddamn Red Sox to the familiar NRA of the National Rifle Association. (Wayne LaPierre, longtime NRA spokesmodel, hails from New Hampshire.) In winter it's trapper caps in plaid, orange, or camouflage; or toques, close-fitting knit caps originally imported from Canada that keep your ears warm and fit under a snowmobile helmet.

Flannel shirts, T-shirts, sweatshirts, insulated vests, and turtle fur are staples for the top half of the fashionable New Hampshirite. Dungarees or Carhartts for the bottom. And no fashionable native would be without at least two pair of overalls, unlined for summer, lined for winter.

And remember, because this is important: Natives do not wear shorts.

Or thongs.

Or trench coats.

Or high heels. You'd break your leg the first hole you stepped in.

Or cowboy boots.

Or cowboy hats.

Or anything to do with cowboys.

No sandals, except with socks thick enough to discourage mosquitoes.

But we will proudly wear just about any item of clothing (except those listed above) procured from the treasure house at the dump, aka "The Country Store." If it's free, it's fashionable. When you tell other natives where you got that purple cardigan with the appliquéd tulips or that pair of button-front, powder-blue polyester slacks, they will be impressed.

Other must-haves for the well-dressed New Hampshire native:

Shoes—Sturdy, brown, tie-up, with good, deep treads.

Bean boots—Leather top, rubber bottom for walking in the wet.

Sorel boots—For hard-core winter use and snowmobiling.

Sneakers—Plain, flat-soled canvas ones, black for men, turquoise for women.

Parka—With a snorkel hood for cold snaps.

Long johns—For an extra layer of warmth in winter and to wear as pajamas year-round.

Flannel wrapper—For wearing over your long johns in case somebody looks in the window while you're watching *Wheel of Fortune* some evening.

Full camouflage suit—For hunting deer with a bow or bird-hunting.

T-shirts—For when it's hot in the summer.

The hunters are sitting around camp. Lucky says: "I'm not gonna be hunting with you fellas next weekend. I told my cousin Dennis I'd go hunting with him over to Grantham. I don't know why I agreed to it. Shouldn't have. He's already shot me twice."

Creepers—To hitch to the bottoms of your boots for walking on ice.

Dark sports coat and dark slacks (men)—For funerals.

Dark dress, skirt, or jumper (women)—For funerals.

The native New Hampshire house

There are also style necessities that distinguish the comfortable and well-decorated New Hampshire home.

Exterior design

Door yard—To park the cars, snowmobiles, tractors, spare culverts, and anything else that doesn't fit in the house, shed, or garage, if you have one.

Backyard—For the swing set, horseshoe pitch, gas grill, and lawn chairs.

Storm windows—To keep out the drafts.

Front door—Never used, just for show.

Side door—For general use.

When Grace raised her hand to speak at town meeting, the long-time moderator said: "Are you a resident?" He knew darned well she was. She lived two doors down from him.

Grace said, "I am, and I have a comment."

The moderator said, "How long have you lived in town?"

Grace said, "Seventeen years, and I'd like to make a comment."

The moderator sighed. "All right," he said, "but keep it short."

Shed—For storage or goats.

Decorative items—Gazing ball, wooden cut-out of a gardener bending over, deer statue so realistic it gets shot at about once a year, toad holding a bowl birdbath.

Exterior covering—Outside walls covered with shingles, clapboards, Tyvek, or, in a pinch, tar paper.

Porch—Screened-in preferred, especially in bug season.

Satellite dish—Required even if you switched over to cable three years ago. We call those big bowls on poles *sculpture*.

Interior design

The decor of each home reflects individual tastes and needs. However, the following can be found in virtually every native abode:

Freezers—At least two, usually three. One with the fridge, one in the back room, one in the garage, if we have one, for storing deer meat and pickerel. We like to keep enough food on hand to last at least six months, in case of emergency.

Woodstoves—At least one, usually two or three. One in the kitchen, one in the main room, one down cellar. And sometimes one in the garage, if we have one. Oil is expensive and winter's long. With wood, even if the electricity goes off, we'll stay warm. (Although, many of us keep a gas generator in the garage, if we have one.)

Large photographs or paintings of ancestors—Our ancestors keep their eyes on us. At Christmas, we paste small, construction-paper Santa hats on Grammie Adah, Grampa Stewart, Aunt Molly and the rest, so they can be part of the festivities.

Inherited furniture and dishes—The old stuff, we believe, is far better than anything you can buy new. And if we haven't inherited it, we buy someone else's treasures at yard sales.

Quilts—We make 'em, we use 'em, and when they wear out, we make some more. Except for the very old ones that have somehow survived the odds. Those we hang on the wall for decoration. And to keep out drafts.

Deer heads with big racks (bonus points for a moose head and rack)—But somebody in the house has to have shot the deer or moose themselves. No fair displaying someone else's kill. That is considered tacky.

6

Towns

New Hampshire has many wonderful small towns to visit, but don't blink. You might miss them. These towns are off the path beaten by our enthusiastic tourism industry, which is what makes them so attractive.

For many of the towns, I've included a story told by a citizen of that town about that town. I believe they're all true to the last comma. Why? Because the tellers told me so.

"This is true story," they say, looking me right in the eye. They all say it. It's a New Hampshire tradition.

Bethlehem

Baby Jesus wasn't born here, but this "Star of the White Mountains" has a lot to recommend it. More than half the town reposes in the White Mountain National Forest, nothing but woods and trails. The Rocks Estate, owned by the Society for the Protection of New Hampshire Forests, features hiking trails, 13 buildings on the National Historic Register, and a working Christmas tree farm, where you can choose your tree, cut it, and drag it out. The Colonial Theater on Main Street is the longest continually running movie house in the country, open every night in the summer.

Driving in Bethlehem, Linda and her family saw a Hassidic Jew, with the long black coat, beard, braids, and wide-brimmed

103

In Woodford, Clark hired Cub to do some plumbing. Clark had lived in town about ten years, so he knew Cub Hardy, a native, was the best plumber around. And he didn't charge an arm and a leg either.

While Cub was under the sink wrestling with the pipes, Clark got a phone call from Ruby White, the selectwoman. Seems Clark had written a letter to the editor in which Ruby felt her integrity had been impugned. Clark tried to explain he meant no such thing. But Ruby was unhappy. She reamed him out but good. Clark couldn't get a word in edgewise.

After he hung up the phone, Clark said: "That Ruby White is a real witch." Only he didn't say witch.

Cub came out from under the sink. "Yup," he said. "That's my sister."

Something to remember about small towns: You don't have to have the same last name to be related.

hat, walking on the side of the road. Linda drove by slowly and, at the stop sign, the Hassid caught up to the car. Her little boy stared at him through the open window. "What?" the Hassid said. "You never saw a Yankee before?"

Candia

At Charmingfare Farm (Route 27), you can get that old-fashioned farm experience, with tractor rides in summer, hay rides in fall, sleigh rides in winter. There's a working dairy barn, a zoo, and a petting area for the animals. The pettable ones anyhow. Among the animals in the zoo are a black bear, cougar, fisher, lynx, swan, porcupine, raccoon, red fox, otter, skunk, trumpeter swan, wolf, and wolverine—not pettable. More pettable: alpacas, cows, donkeys, horses, llamas, sheep, rabbits, goats, and pigs.

This story came to me from a woman in Candia several years ago. She was a woman with some age to her. She used a walker and pulled oxygen on wheels along with her.

She said: "My mother-in-law was a real pistol. A lot of people don't get along with their in-laws, but Betty and I always got along good. After my father-in-law died, naturally I went to the calling hours, and there he was, all laid out in the casket. Betty was standing by the head. I went over to her. She says, 'How do you think he looks?' I said, 'Good.' She said, 'What do you think of his tie?' I said, 'It's a nice tie, Betty. Elegant.' She said, 'I bought that tie for him three Christmases ago. He never wore it. By god, he's going to wear it now.'"

Cornish

The Catcher in the Rye. You read it. We all did. Maybe you read J. D. Salinger's short stories, too. Maybe you're wondering when he's going to publish a new book since the last one came out in 1965. So why not stop by his house and ask him? Salinger has lived in Cornish since 1953. Ask anybody in town where he lives and THEY WON'T TELL YOU. Salinger likes his privacy and New Hampshirites respect that.

What's he doing out there in the woods all by himself? Some say on a quiet evening, you can hear the sound of typewriter keys being struck. Others think he's watching *America's Next Top Model* and carving little dolls out of clothespins. Whatever J. D. Salinger is up to, New Hampshirites agree, it's none of our damn business.

One of J. D. Salinger's tight-mouthed Cornish neighbors had a problem. Somebody was sneaking out to the woodpile in the night and siphoning off cordwood a few sticks at a time. So the neighbor drilled a hole in a piece from the stack, filled the hole with black powder, and plugged the hole good. He placed the rigged piece right where he could find it again. Didn't want to use it by mistake and blow up his own woodstove. He scratched out a note: "Steal at your own risk. One stick is stuffed with black powder."

Which solved the problem, sort of. Next time the fella checked his woodpile, it was just as he left it, except the note had been altered. The ONE crossed out, and TWO written in its place.

Dublin

The home of *Yankee* magazine and *The Old Farmer's Almanac*, the paperback with the hole punched in the corner so it can be hung on a nail in the outhouse for easy reading. You can see the collection of red buildings in downtown Dublin where the magazine has been published since 1935. If you want a sneak peek, go to www.almanac.com and click on the webcam. It shows *Yankee* headquarters in real time.

If you're a fan of *Yankee* and a regular reader of Edie Clark's column, "The View from Mary's Farm," you might want to take a ride on some of the back roads of Dublin. The scenery's woodsy, the houses old and well maintained, and stone walls abundant. If you don't find Mary's exact farm, you'll find others much like it.

Just outside of town on Route 137 North, Del Rossi's Trattoria serves good Italian food and hosts poetry readings. This has been going on for twenty years. Each fall (Autumn Oracles) and spring (Writes of Spring) on selected Sundays, "audiences gather to hear poets and writers reclaim the language from the page as they tell their stories in the ancient oral tradition of the

bards." I've told stories at Del Rossi's
and felt the spirit of the Bard within
me. That's right. I've also felt the
Maiale e Melanzane alla Parmigiana
within me, and it was delicious.
(That's breaded scaloppine of bone-
less pork loin and roasted eggplant,
oven-broiled with tomato-basil
sauce, asiago parmesan, and moz-
zarella cheese, served with home-
made spaghetti pomodoro.)

Once a year The Milton
Ensemble performs at Del Rossi's.
This group of writers, actors, and
scholars "has dedicated itself to rein-

The debate at town meeting was whether to continue to pay some hundreds of dollars a year to run electricity to the eight streetlights lining Main Street. The lights were old and needed replacing. Why not just shut them down? A voter said, "Without the streetlights, how would strangers know they'd passed through town?"

venting the way *Paradise Lost* is presented to the contemporary
audience." Director Rodger Martin says, "We get it off the page
into the air as a dramatic reading, and suddenly the listener is
transported away from footnotes and allusion to one of the
great stories of the English language." The Ensemble's goal is to
record and perform each book from *Paradise Lost* much as Milton
intended in the 17th century—as a masque or choral reading.

To date, they have performed and recorded nine of the
twelve books from the epic poem, and 2008 is the 400th
anniversary of Milton's birth.

New Hampshirites love Milton, especially Satan, the original
Free Stater.

At a Dublin town meeting, the question of whether the
monies taken in from the selling of cemetery plots should be
put into a trust fund led to a lengthy discussion. During this
discussion, one of the assembled, new to town, asked about the

process of buying one. What did a person have to do to get a lot?

The cemetery trustee said: "I'll tell you one thing—you can't just come in cold."

Effingham

We include Effingham only because it's our favorite town name. It's our favorite town name because you can say things like:

"Where'd you have your accident, Sid?"

"Hit an effin' patch of black effin' ice in effin' Effin'ham and slid into the effin' ditch."

This story dates back to Prohibition. One dark, rainy night—true story—a long black sedan got bogged down in the mud, and this was right in the village, right on the main drag. Wainwright Adams heard the wheels spinning, the crying and cursing and so forth. He raised himself out of bed. Pulled on his pants and overcoat. Thirty minutes later, with the help of some planks, sawdust, and a good deal of pushing and grunting, the sedan was free. The four men in suits and fedoras appreciated Wain's help. One of them handed him a ten-dollar bill, which was a lot of money in those days.

In the lantern light, Wain couldn't help but notice some

Charter went down the road to visit his neighbor, a farmer in Barrington. He found the farmer in the barn with a bucket of slop, feeding his big sow Prudence with a teaspoon. The farmer would dip the teaspoon into the bucket, hold it to Prudence's snout, and she'd lick it clean. Then they'd repeat the process.

"Don't it take a long time to feed that pig with a teaspoon?" Charter said.

The farmer replied, "Time don't mean nothing to a pig."

blemishes in the finish of that long black sedan. More than blemishes, they looked like bullet holes, eight or ten of them. The driver saw Wain looking those bullet holes over, kind of googly-eyed. "Don't worry," the man said. "Those aren't from the police. They're from our competition."

Jeesum, Wain thought. Rumrunners.

He pocketed the $10, and the rumrunners went on their merry way.

Later, when he told the story, he always added, "I thought it best not to mention that I was the constable."

Epping

At the New England Dragway, you can test your skill with a car, a motorcycle, or a snowmobile, so long as you have a driver's license, and—on Wednesday and Friday nights—a muffler. Helmets are encouraged. Grudge race? This is the place. It's also the place for the International Hot Rod Association's North American Nationals. Open four days a week, April through October; let the rev of engines and the squeal of tires ring out over Epping!

Daniel Webster Harvey, Epping native and raconteur, is chuck full of stories. (*Raconteur* is French for "chuck full of stories.") Here's one:

"The old maid got a proposal. 'Oh,' she said, 'this is so sudden.'"

Errol

The bull moose in L.L. Cote Sports Center in downtown Errol is massive, stuffed, and white. **FYI:** Most moose are

brown. Once you've seen the moose, shop around. L.L. Cote
has a great selection of outdoorsy clothes, chain saws, woodstoves, hot tubs, snowblowers, canoes and kayaks, fishing
equipment, archery supplies, camping gear, knives, and guns.
They rent snowmobiles and ATVs as well. It's one-stop shopping just a hop, skip, and a jump from Lake Umbagog.

Going ice fishing, the fellas were driving across the Umbagog,
their jeep heavy-loaded with equipment and supplies from L.L.
Cote's—augers, buckets, tackle, shiners—and the obligatory
cooler of beer and hot dogs. Bert noticed a 20-foot length of
rope hanging off the back of the jeep and a 1-gallon plastic
milk container attached to the end. It bounced along the ice as
they went. "What's that for?" he asked his buddies.

"That's so if we go through the ice, the milk jug will float,
and they'll know where to find us."

Fitzwilliam

The rhododendrons bloom in late July, 16 acres of them,
and some of them 30 feet high. This is about as far north as
rhododendrons can stand the cold. The patch by the "Old Patch
House" might have been lost to lumbering except for the con-
cern and generosity of Mary Lee Ware, who bought the land in
1902 and deeded it to the Applachian Mountain Club to be
protected and open to the public. And, she added, no rhodie
would ever be picked, and no ax used on the trees. She was a
stickler.

Years ago, Logan had a farm on a back road in the lowlands
of Fitzwilliam. Every once in a while, somebody from away
would get their vehicle stuck in a mud hole out in front of the
farm house. Logan kept his tractor handy for pulling them out.

110

He didn't ask much, but wouldn't turn away a ten-spot if offered. The tourist paid the ten dollars, grateful to be back on the road. Logan said: "Gawd, seems like I spend half my time pulling fellas like you out of that mud hole."

"What do you do the other half of the time?" the tourist asked.

"Haul in the water."

I asked a longtime resident of Orange what the population was. She said with confidence, "Three hundred and seven." Then her brow furrowed. "No," she said, "the Brown girl had twins and the Johnsons moved to Canaan. So it's three hundred and five." She poured my tea. "Oh!" she said, "and my husband died last year. So we're down to three hundred four."

Haverhill

Front and center of the postcard-pretty village common is Alumni Hall, Cultural and Interpretive Center, complete with four white pillars and a cupola. In the 1800s it was the Grafton Country Courthouse, and later served as the Haverhill Academy auditorium and gym. Now it's a grand place to hold an auction, an art show, a benefit concert, or even for a story-teller to spin her tales. (Yup, that was me.)

But wait, there's more. In the South Common, you'll find the Museum of American Weather. Well, not all American weather. This museum devotes itself to the blizzard of 1888, the flood of 1927, the hurricane of 1938, and one tornado in Worcester. In New Hampshire, we love weather!

But wait, there's still more. Don't miss the Haverhill-Bath covered bridge, built in 1829 and in use through 1999. It's the oldest covered bridge in the country, on the National Register of Historic Places. And like everything else, it always needs upkeep. The Haverhill-Bath Covered Bridge Committee takes care of that. In New Hampshire, we love our covered bridges. Covered bridges don't freeze first.

Miss Patti Page, "The Singing Rage," made over 100 albums, 160 singles, and had 84 Top 40 Billboard Hits. She's a Grammy winner. Remember "Mockin' Bird Hill," "Tennessee Waltz," and "How Much Is that Doggie in the Window?" She still performs 50 or so concerts a years. She lives at Hilltop Farm in Bath, where she produces maple products, like "Patti's Syrup that Sings."

Henniker

Famous for being the only Henniker in the world, it's the birthplace of Amy Marcy Cheney Beach, a child prodigy who lived from 1867–1944, and composed more than 150 published works—choral, orchestral, sacred, and songs. At age four, while visiting her grandfather, she composed her first piano pieces, four waltzes. In her head. Her grandfather had no piano. She played them for her astonished mother when she got home. Amy Beach wrote many of her later works during summers at the MacDowell Colony in Peterborough. She had a warm relationship with the playwright Thornton Wilder and, of an evening, would cheer on her friend, the poet Edwin Arlington Robinson, as he played billiards.

You can find out more about Amy at the Henniker Historical Society Museum, Academy Hall, 51 Maple Street, right next to the Congregational Church.

Henniker is also home to New England College.

Littleton

Littleton's a pretty big town, population nearly 6,000. Downright urban, for the North Country. The Village Bookstore is a destination in itself, two floors of books, maps, music, and toys. Peruse the League of New Hampshire Craftsmen gallery next door. Or grab a sandwich at Miller's Cafe and Bakery in the restored grist mill on Mill Street next to the covered walking bridge across the scenic Ammonoosuc River.

You could blink two or three times and not miss busy downtown Littleton with the river running through it.

But you might miss Pollyanna if you're not looking sharp. The bronze statue was sculpted by New Hampshire artist Emile Birch. The relentlessly cheerful child stands on the front lawn of the library, her bronze arms open wide, a broad-brimmed bronze hat shading her smiling bronze face as her bronze skirts swirl about her. Rubbing her boots is said to be good luck.

Why Pollyanna? Why Littleton? Eleanor H. Porter, the author of the popular 1913 novel, lived here.

Each year on a Saturday in June, Littleton celebrates "Glad Day," in honor of Pollyanna. There is a parade and the whole town smiles—all day long. It's mandatory.

In Littleton, they call Pollyanna "New Hampshire's Most Welcoming Attraction."

Mason

Uncle Sam—that's right, the guy with the pointing finger and top hat all decked out in red, white, and blue—grew up in Mason. Sam Wilson made his fortune in meat, and he always marked his shipping barrels u.s. for, well, the U.S. But then folks started associating it with our own U. S.—Uncle Sam

Live Free and Eat Pie!

Top Ten New Hampshire Souvenirs

(prices may vary)

1) Stuffed moose embroidered with I MISS MY OLD MAN on his plush chest. $9.99

2) Great Stone Face tie in red, blue or gray. $24

3) Granite paperweight embossed with the state seal. $24

4) Live Free or Die sippy cup. $6.95

5) Gold-plated Concord Coach Christmas tree ornament. $17

6) A pound of Snappy Old Cheese purchased from Joel at Calef's Country Store in Barrington. (Price fluctuates depending on milk supply; tell Joel I sent you and he might cut you a deal.)

7) A gallon of pure, grade-A, medium amber maple syrup. $40 to infinity (depending on how the sap ran this year)

8) Mini balsam pillow, embossed with a moose and stuffed with fragrant pine needles. $3.99

9) Fritz Wetherbee's *Speak N'Hampsha Like a Native* CD. Nobody speaks N'Hampsha like Fritz, star of *New Hampshire Chronicle* on WMUR. He'll teach you how to approximate the lingo, though even Fritz will admit, no one except a native can truly speak like a native. It's an art. $12.99

10) Segway Human Transporter invented by New Hampshire's own Dean Kamen, who also invented the stair-climbing wheelchair and the portable insulin pump. Eighty million dollars went into designing and producing these gyro-scooters. You stand on them and they respond to the tip and tilt of your body, always in balance. They move right along fast, too. The original asking price of $5,000 seemed cheap enough, but I found several on eBay for under $3,000. Segway—the ultimate New Hampshire souvenir.

Wilson. He became a national symbol during the War of 1812 when illustrator Thomas Nast used him as a model for political cartoons.

Don't blink or you'll miss Wilson's childhood home on Route 123. A historic marker with highlights of his life marks the spot.

For more Uncle Sam information, the Mason Historical Society sells a pamphlet called "The Story of Uncle Sam" by Elizabeth Orton Jones.

Nelson

People have been dancing in Nelson for more than 200 years. For the last few decades, they've been contra dancing every Monday night at the town hall, usually to the music of Harvey Tolman, master fiddler. So join hands, circle left, box the gnat, then make a chain! You'll catch on quick. If you don't, smile and fake it.

Harvey Tolman himself told me these stories. He's a treasure really. He received the Governor's Folk Heritage Award for excellent folk heritage and good fiddling.

Harvey recalled a Nelson town meeting, when the debate concerned how much hose to buy for the fire department. After a lot of back-and-forth, a citizen said: "Why don't we wait for a fire, then see how much we're short."

He also recalled a local who had three holes cut in the wall of the back shed, off the kitchen. "What are those holes for?" Harvey asked.

"For the cats." The man had three cats.

"Why can't the cats all use one hole?"

"Because when I say skat, I mean *skat*."

Newbury

I'm often asked if I'm one of the Chicken Rock Rules. No relation, but the story goes like this. A family of Rules lived and raised chickens on Route 103 near a big rock with a flat face. A young man in town, head over heels in love with young Gretchen Rule, proclaimed his passion by spray-painting CHICKEN FARMER I LOVE YOU on the rock face.

Word is that Gretchen didn't exactly fall for it. But the message stayed, a reminder to all who drive Route 103 that romance thrives. Even in New Hampshire. A couple of decades after the first incarnation, the weathered message was repainted: CHICKEN FARMER I STILL LOVE YOU, it said.

Years passed. Somebody complained. Probably a stickler. This was graffiti and should be removed! The Department of Transportation erased the love letter. In less than a week, the message reappeared, bigger and brighter than ever, CHICKEN FARMER I STILL LOVE YOU.

And there it stays, a testimony to enduring, if unrequited, love.

Nottingham

Cedar Waters Nudist Camp off Route 125 is among the country's oldest (since 1950) and biggest (350 acres including a lake) family-friendly nudist colonies: no singles, no same-sex couples, no alchohol on-site—just good nude Christian family fun. Activities include tennis, shuffleboard, horseshoes, and volleyball. Swimming, of course.

Ida asked if I'd seen all the boats headed toward the big beach at the east end of our lake. "I did," I told her. I'd seen a

116

whole bunch of them—canoes and kayaks, too—all loaded with camping equipment.

"A few of them had big blue barrels," I said to Ida.

"Those weren't barrels," she said. "Those were kegs. All those people went down to the big beach and set up camp. Claude and I took a ride by in the boat. You wouldn't believe it. Those people were drinking and singing and dancing and carousing. They had a big fire going, music blaring. They had a volleyball net set up and they were hollering and swearing and jumping around."

"Quite a party," I said.

"Yuh," she said, "once those nudists get going, you don't know what's going to happen."

Pittsburg

Our northernmost town, Pittsburg was once a sovereign nation, "The Indian Stream Republic" (1832–1835).

The largest brown trout on record, 16 lbs. 6 oz., came out of the Connecticut River in Pittsburg. The whopper was caught in 1975 by Ken Reed Jr., from Connecticut, the state. Yes, it's true. The man who caught the biggest brown trout ever was not even a native.

Which Pittsburg(h) am I?

How do you know whether you're in Pittsburg, New Hampshire, or Pittsburgh, Pennsylvania? (Answers at bottom of page. Don't peek.)

1) I have an "h" at the end of my name and a football team called the Steelers.

2) One of my big tourist attractions is Moose Alley.

3) My population density is three persons per square mile.

4) For sport, I host six hunting seasons—bear, moose, deer, duck, turkey, and out-a-staters. Actually, when you break down deer season into bow, muzzleloader, and rifle seasons, it's nine seasons.

5) The nearest interstate highway is 57 miles away.

6) Public transportation? None. Unless you count calling Cousin Minnie for a lift, which I wouldn't recommend until she's healed up from having her cataracts peeled.

7) One of the top recreational activities: Combing the woods for antlers to add to the collection.

8) I'm a big city in Pennsylvania.

9) Among my fine dining establishments is the Buck Rub Pub at the Connecticut Lakes Lodge, where you can buy a 12-inch Buck Rub steak bomb for $6.00 (price subject to change).

10) I was named after an English guy named William Pitt.

Answers: # 1 and 8 Pennsylvania. #10 Both! All the rest, New Hampshire.

Salisbury

Besides having one of the most picturesque town centers of all the picturesque town centers in the state, Salisbury is the site of the Daniel Webster Birthplace. Daniel Webster was, of course, a famous orator and statesman in the early 1800s. In Stephen Vincent Benet's short story, "The Devil and Daniel Webster," he outfoxes the foxiest and beats Satan at his own game.

The Birthplace, run by the state parks department, is open weekends from Memorial Day until Labor Day. For $3 (free if you're under 17 or over 65), you can tour the house, furnished

as it would have been back in the day, with its original fireplace
and hearth of handmade bricks.

Controversy: Some—including the state parks department—
claim the Daniel Webster Birthplace is in Franklin. In fact, the
town of Salisbury was incorporated as part of Franklin in 1828.
But now it's Salisbury again. What is that about? All I know is
when I was a kid, about once a year my parents would take us
for a ride out 127 to see the Daniel Webster Birthplace. We
never stopped. We just drove by slow. We'd go by the old
Salisbury cemetery, past the house where the lady had lots of
cats, and there it'd be—Daniel Webster Birthplace. In
Salisbury.

Sutton

Muster Field Farm Museum is a restored 18th-century
homestead and working farm, with 250 acres of fields and
woods, gardens, hiking, crosscountry skiing, and snowshoeing.
It's open year-round and hosts special events from time to
time, including a Civil War encampment in the summer, a
Harvest Day in the Fall, and Ice Day in January.

On Ice Day, the ice men and women cometh. They cut
blocks with big long ice saws on Kezar Lake, pull them out
with a fulcrum, and haul them to the icehouse at Muster Field
Farm. It's a chilly business, but stacked and covered with sawdust, the ice will last through summer.

Check the web site for more information: www. muster-
fieldfarm.com.

In the 1800s and early 1900s, when everybody's ice came
from lakes, not freezers, New Hampshire ice harvesters would

stack the blocks on the trains to sell in Boston, and stack the tourists on the same cars for the ride back. Worked out good.

Wakefield

The Museum of Childhood in the historic district of Wakefield displays dolls and toys (old and new), and a re-creation of a one-room schoolhouse from 1890. Best of all, it houses a section of Mr. Pearl's sled, the biggest double-runner sled in the world. It was 77 feet long and could carry as many as 70 riders, if they liked each other. Loaded and with the snow just right, it would get going so fast that when the one in front screamed, the one in back never heard it.

Mr. Pearl called his sled "Uncle Sam," and gave many a coasting party for local children in Farmington, where he lived.

In January of 1895, Mr. Pearl, who always steered, took 70 people for a ride down Farmington's hilly, icy Main Street, coasting 700 plus feet and winning a barrel of apples and an oyster supper for the whole crew.

Some sled. Some ride.

Walpole

L.A. Burdick Handmade Chocolates makes premium artisan candies out of chocolate imported from France, Switzerland, and Venezuela. The hot chocolate served at the restaurant in downtown Walpole is so thick your spoon stands up in it. (Been there; done it.) The bonbons are shaped by hand. In the gift shop, chunks of broken chocolate are dished out for tasting. They taste good. L.A. Burdick ships their famous chocolates all over the world. Check out www.burdickchocolate.com.

Ken Burns, the filmmaker (*The Civil War, Baseball, Jazz*), lives in Walpole. He likes chocolate.

Warren

Centered on the town green is a Jupiter-C rocket, like the one Alan Shepard Jr. of Derry went into space on. But this is not a space travel vehicle; it's an expired Redstone missile, disarmed, of course. It weighs 8 tons and stands 70 feet high, taller than any of the buildings in the vicinity. The nearby historical society houses a collection of space-related memorabilia, including a letter from astronaut Shepard.

While you're in Warren, stop at the New Hampshire State Fish Hatchery on Route 25 at the south end of town. It's open to the public seven days a week. You can watch the fish, some small, some big. Maybe they'll even let you feed them.

Waterville Valley

Curious George lived in Waterville Valley. He summered there, anyway. Margret and H. A. Rey, author of the books about the monkey and the man in the yellow hat, owned a home on Village Road. For information about programming, events, monkeyshines, and antics at the Curious George Cottage, check www.reycenter.org.

Wilmot

Wilmot is home to one of New Hampshire's most acclaimed writers, Donald Hall. He is a former United States Poet Laureate and he writes often about Eagle Pond and Kearsarge

Mountain, both of which happen to be in Wilmot. He was married to Jane Kenyon, also a famous poet, but she died.

Kearsarge Mountain makes a great family climb. It's only 2,937 feet high, but the view is spectacular because it stands alone. The trail from Winslow State Park, the Wilmot side, is more challenging than the trail from Rollins State Park on the Warner side. On the Warner side you can drive more than halfway to the top. From the Wilmot side, you walk the whole way.

A neighbor heard the old fella up the road was ailing, so she took him a casserole. He thanked her. A week later, she went back to collect her dish. "How'd you like the casserole?" she asked.

He replied: "It wa'n't up to Wilmot standards."

Moral of the story: Be careful when you ask a native for his opinion. He will give it.

7

Attractions

In New Hampshire we love our glacial erratics so
much we name them: Frog Rock, Madison Boulder, Boise Rock,
Pulpit Rock, Goodrich Rock, Davis Boulder, Glen Boulder,
Index Rock, Vessel Rock, Sucker Brook Rock, Flat Top Rock, Big
Bumpy Rock, Pyramid Rock, Big Bob, Little Bob, Elvis.

Glacial erratic means big rock in an odd place, kind of off by
itself, dropped by the glacier as it passed through a long time
ago. New Hampshire has always had a lot of big rocks, erratic
and otherwise. We study them. We see things in them. On the
side of Cannon Mountain, we saw a cannon. We also saw the
profile of an old man, which became our state symbol. Dewey
Rock on Artist Bluff in Franconia looks exactly like Admiral
George Dewey, right down to the mole on his right cheek. It's
eerie. Most of our rocks are granite, which is why we're called
The Granite State.

Matter of fact, my father grew up in the shadow of a glacial
erratic in Danbury. In the family story, my grandmother,
Elizabeth Moynihan Barker, was home alone at the one-room
cabin when a brush salesman showed up. He was making small
talk, you know, buttering her up. He took a look at that big rock
towering over the cabin and wondered how it came to be there.

"I don't know," said my grandmother, Elizabeth Moynihan
Barker, in her Irish brogue. "T'was here when I arrived."

Maren's Rock was a big rock by the shore just like any other until a fateful night in 1873 when Anethe Christensen and her sister-in-law Karen Christensen were murdered with an ax. Maren Hontvet, Karen's younger sister, told the grisly tale of a bloodthirsty intruder. She had narrowly escaped being murdered herself.

The story made national news when Celia Thaxter—poet, essayist, and resident of a neighboring island—wrote it up in all its gruesome detail for *The Atlantic Monthly*. Louis Wagner, who had once boarded with the family, was accused, arrested, and hung for the murders. Evidently, he rowed 10 miles out to the Shoals, then 10 miles back in the middle of the night, murdered Anethe and Karen, but couldn't find Maren, who escaped the house, ran to the rock, and hid there all night clutching her dog for warmth.

But . . . through the years some have questioned Maren's version of the story. In *The Weight of Water*, Anita Shreve posited that Maren herself was the killer, jealous of lovely young Anethe and sick of toothless Karen's carping. Others thought maybe Maren's husband John sneaked back from an overnight fishing trip to do in his annoying relatives. Maybe Maren and John were in it together. Or maybe Celia Thaxter's son, known to have some mental problems, sneaked off his island, popped over to Smuttynose, and did the deed. And Celia was covering up for him!

Could be. You hear different things.

They were all here when we arrived. And, barring road construction and Holiday Inns, they'll be here after we're gone. Maybe it's the permanence of these rocks that's so appealing.

My dad had a saying when he was splitting rocks, something he did a lot of because to add on to our house he had to dig into the bony hill behind it. He'd chisel away at the hardpan for a while, then hit rock, once again proving out the New Hampshire motto: "It'll go along like this for a while, then it'll get worse." When he hit a real big rock, he'd say: "I may not be able to outmuscle this rock, and I know I won't outlive it, but I'm pretty sure I can outsmart it."

In Iowa they grow corn. In Maine they grow potatoes. In New Hampshire we grow rocks. In an old story, a farmer is working in his field in Orford. A passerby asks what he's up to. The farmer says: "Picking rocks and piling 'em."

"Where'd all those rocks come from?" the passerby asks.

"Well," the farmer says, "the glacier brought 'em."

"Where's the glacier now?"

"Guess it went back for another load."

Top fourteen rocks and rock formations

The Old Man of the Mountain, Franconia Notch

Deceased but preserved on the New Hampshire quarter, road signs, postcards, paintings, and even as a bobblehead.

Indian Head profile, Mount Pemigewasset

Looks like the profile of an American Indian and is best seen from near the Indian Head Resort in Lincoln. It was in the shadow of the Indian Head that Betty and Barney Hill were abducted by aliens in 1961.

Madison Boulder, Madison

One of the biggest glacial erratics in the world, the Madison Boulder is located off Route 113. It's really big, bigger than my house. I'm not kidding. It weighs more than 5,000 tons, and measures more than 80 feet long, nearly 40 feet through, and 23 feet high, and that's just what's above ground.

Cathedral Ledge, Bartlett and North Conway

The top is in Bartlett, the base in North Conway off Route 16/302. You can drive up for a hair-raising view of Echo Lake and surrounds. You can walk along the trail at the top, but don't slip or that'll be the end of you. Some people climb the 700 feet nearly straight up from the bottom using crampons and other tools. Some climb the ledge in the winter. On the ice. We have a special name for those people. We call them Nuts.

Maren's Rock, Smuttynose

Smuttynose is one of the Isles of Shoals off our 13-mile coastline. Maren's Rock is named for Maren Hontvet, who escaped an ax murderer by hiding in the shelter of the rock. You can catch a ride to the Shoals with the Isles of Shoals Steamship Company on Market Street in Portsmouth. It's about a 45-minute ride one way.

Boulder Field, Pawtuckaway State Park

You walk out through the piney woods a good ways and come upon these monoliths among the trees holding a rock convention, some of them 30 feet high. They don't say much. They just stand there, reminiscent—if you squint—of those big statues on Easter Island. The main entrance to Pawtuckaway, which has a beach and lots of trails for hiking and mountain-biking, is off Routh 156 in Nottingham.

Frog Rock (A), New Boston

Actually, it sits almost exactly on the line between New Boston and Mont Vernon. It's big and it looks like a frog. Some say it looks more like a toad, because it's bumpy, suggesting warts. If you press your ear to Frog Rock's lips, you can hear him whispering "Live free or croak."

126

Frog Rock (B), Moultonborough

This frog rock is about a tenth the size of the New Boston ersatz amphibian. This croaker is located on Route 109 between Moultonborough and Tuftonboro. To enhance the frog effect, local artists have painted him green. They painted two eyes as well, in case you're confused about which end is which.

Elephant's Head, Crawford Notch

You can see it from Route 302, or take a hike on the Webster-Jackson Trail for a closer look.

Mount Forist, Berlin

This is the whole elephant. Viewed from the East Side of Berlin (Mount Forist is on the West Side), you can see the trunk, head, back, belly, and rump of the elephant. My friend Norman Greene, giving directions to his house, told me I'd find him under the belly of the elephant. Sure enough, there he was!

The Old Lady of the Mountain, Franconia Notch

The Old Man's gone but the Old Lady remains. She's also called "The Watcher." You can watch the watcher from the

Full disclosure: Some of the Isles of Shoals are in Maine. Maine's got zillions of islands all up and down its zig-zag coast. New Hampshire has just the Shoals, and only half of them. You'd think Maine could be a little bit magnanimous in the Shoals department.

Technically, Smuttynose lies on the Maine side of the watery boundary. But that boundary has always been iffy. Maine claims the Portsmouth Naval Shipyard, despite the fact that Portsmouth is in New Hampshire. Over the years, lawsuits have been filed disputing Maine's claim to the yard. So far, it's still in Maine—but you never know. Flood comes and the Piscataqua shifts a few feet one way or the other, those shipyard workers won't be paying any more Maine state income tax.

Mountain Trivia

Number of peaks equal to or over 4,000 feet:

Vermont:	5
Maine:	14
New Hampshire:	48
Massachusetts, Rhode Island or Connecticut:	0
Holland:	0

Peaks above 5,000 feet:

New Hampshire:	7
Maine:	1
Vermont:	0

south end of Profile Lake. She's hanging off the side of Mount Lafayette.

The Flume Gorge, Mount Liberty

A brook cut the gorge creating granite walls 90 feet high in places. For hundreds, maybe thousands of years, a boulder sat stuck precariously between the narrow walls way up high, but in 1883, the boulder washed away in a torrent.

Glen Boulder, Pinkham Notch

As seen from Route 16 in Pinkham Notch, this boulder looks like it's about to roll off the side of the mountain, but there it stays, like a marble on a steeple. Though, on closer inspection, it looks more like an upside-down boot.

Vessel Rock, Gilsum

Vessel Rock doesn't look nearly as much like a ship under full sail as it did before the bow and jib fell off. Still, it's quite a rock, more than 40 feet long, 30 feet wide and 25 feet high. It sits close to Vessel Rock Road and closer still to a small, privately owned house, not far from Vessel Rock Cemetery.

America's Stonehenge, Salem

Also known as Mystery Hill, these megalithic rocks are a big calendar, built by . . . who knows? in the year . . . we're not sure? That's the mystery. On the 30 hilly acres, somebody put up some primitive buildings, walls, and stone piles, and made some tunnels. One slab rock is called the Sacrificial Stone, but nobody really knows if any sacrificing was ever done here. What's the difference between America's Stonehenge and the Stonehenge in England? This one's in New Hampshire and the rocks are smaller.

Attractions besides rocks

Contrary to what you might think, the Granite State is not all about rocks. There are many wonderful non-rock attractions as well. Of course, you'll want to hit the high spots, Mount Washington being the highest. Take the Cog up. You'll want to drive the Kancamagus Highway, cruise Lake Winnipesaukee on the *Mount Washington*, shop Market Square in downtown Portsmouth, then walk through Prescott Park to Strawbery Banke to see what colonial New England looked like and learn why both *Strawbery* and *Banke* are misspelled. You'll check out the world-class Currier Museum of Art in Manchester, take a whale-watch boat out of Rye, visit the State House in Concord to bask

in the glow of its golden dome and check out the Concord
Coach. You'll take a tour of the Anheuser-Busch Brewery in
Merrimack and sample the wares. You must take a Moose Tour in
Moose Alley, departing from Gorham. You look at the moose;
the moose look at you. The kids will want to visit Santa's Village
and Six Gun City in Jefferson, and Story Land in Glen. None of
these kids' destinations are anything like Disney World. And
we're thankful for that. They're small, by comparison. They're
quaint, by comparison. Around here we call that *charm*.

The Cog

In the 1860s when Sylvester Marsh asked permission to
build a railroad to the top of Mount Washington, the legislators
down to Concord thought his idea was so ridiculous, they said:
"Go ahead—build a railway to the moon for all we care."

The Rock Pile is famous for being in the fog. Up top, you're
lucky if you can see your hand in front of your face. The day my
husband, John, and I took a Cog ride, we were lucky. Not only
could we see our hands, but all over. On a clear day, you can
see four states, Quebec, and the Atlantic Ocean. We couldn't
see the ocean, but got some grand views of the Whites and way
beyond.

Martin, our brakeman, gave us a brief history on the ride up
and answered questions. A wiry young man with a goatee, his
railroad cap was dark with soot, as was his uniform—dark
work pants and shirt with his name embroidered on it. Soot
floated in through the windows and dusted us all.

"What was your most memorable trip?" I asked, hoping he'd
had a dangerous encounter with a bear or a celebrity like
Martha Stewart. Nope. His most memorable trips were "when
we break down," he said.

130

He didn't elaborate.

Somebody asked if lightning ever struck the rails, three miles of exposed steel on the side of a mountain.

"Yup," Martin said.

As we pulled to a side track to let another train pass, he advised us to "take pictures of the tourists taking pictures." Sure enough, the folks on the other train leaned out the windows to take pictures of us. And vice versa.

Someone asked if Martin encountered much wildlife on these trips. "Sure," he said. "Deer, foxes, coyotes, moose."

The moose, he told us, will run alongside the track, looking back every once in a while to see if the train is still coming. They'll run until they're frothing at the mouth. Then, and only then, does the idea bulb turn on: "I could run into the woods and get away from this great, noisy, smoke-belching monster." Which the moose proceeds to do.

Why New Hampshire has no sales tax

A few decades back William Loeb, the powerful, outspoken, and very conservative publisher of our biggest newspaper, the *Manchester Union Leader,* declared that no one should be elected in New Hampshire unless he or she took the anti-tax pledge—specifically, no broad-based taxes like a sales tax or income tax.

New Hampshire candidates have been taking the pledge ever since. And those who don't . . . lose. Is this a good thing?

Seems pretty good. Until you have to pay your property tax.

One time, Martin said, an engineer got into a bit of difficulty. When he went to suit up, the clean uniforms hadn't come back, so he had to put on yesterday's shirt and pants, dirty with oil and kerosene from maintenance work. It was a cold day—gets awful cold on Mount Washington. Worst weather in the world! And proud of it. To warm himself, the engineer cozied up to the firebox. As Martin's train passed the engineer's, Martin noticed that the man's pants were on fire, and the engineer was doing his darnedest to extinguish his flaming bum. "Lucky he had his longjohns on," Martin said.

By tradition, hikers on Mount Washington moon the Cog as it passes. Near the top, the trails pass right under the raised tracks. If a mooning should occur, Martin said, you've got two choices: "Look away. Or get out your camera."

I got out my camera.

You can catch the Cog on the Base Road at Bretton Woods. Go to www.thecog.com for directions, schedules, and ticket prices.

Concord Coach

Many states, including Massachusetts, Texas, and North Carolina, have Concords, but only ours is a state capital. Appropriately, *concord* means agreement or harmony, which is what our state legislature, the third-largest legislative body in the world, aspires to. We pronounce our Concord, *conkid*, *conkurd*, or *concud*. North Carolina pronounces its Concord, *con-cord*, like the grape. In North Carolina they say: "We're Con-cord; we've never been Conquered."

New Hampshire's Concord is the birthplace of the Concord Coach, built by Abbot-Downing Company in the mid-1800s. The Concord Coach conquered the West by making travel over the Overland Stage Trail Route comfy as could be. When you see the horse-drawn stage careening across the desert, chased by bandits or Indians in movies starring John Wayne, that's likely a Concord Coach, the height of luxury at the time, sort of like that wide-beamed Concord airplane that used to fly back and forth to France very fast.

You can see an honest-to-goodness Concord Coach in the lobby of the Concord Monitor building on One Monitor Drive. In the summer there's one on display at the Sandwich Fairgrounds Museum, another at Six Gun City in Jefferson, and one at The Flume in Franconia Notch. Other coaches come out of the barn for parades. For $35 you can order the plans for a Concord Coach from the Oregon Historical Society Press and build your own.

Currier Museum of Art

In downtown Manchester at 192 Orange Street, the Currier Museum of Art has lots of art and a nice cafe. The American collection includes work by Thomas Cole, Albert Bierstadt, Arthur Dove, and Marsden Hartley. The Europeans are represented by Claude Monet, Pablo Picasso, and Henri Matisse, among others.

Take the shuttle from the museum for a one-hour guided tour of the Zimmerman House, fully furnished and designed by Frank Lloyd Wright in 1950. It's cool.

Kancamagus Highway

Hard to spell, harder to pronounce, we call it the Kank. This scenic highway from Lincoln in the west to Conway in the east is listed by GORP as one of the top-ten mountain drives in the country. The two-lane byway runs 35 miles through the White Mountain National Forest. At its highest point, you're 2,355 feet above sea level and your ears will be popping. Great mountain views. Great river views. Lots of places to picnic. No houses, just woods. And moose. And tourists.

Ruggles Mine

This "Mine in the Sky" on Isinglass Mountain in Grafton was a working mica mine from 1803 until 1959. *Isinglass* means mica, and it used to be used for window glass, especially in wood- and coal stoves. Besides mica, the mine produced feldspar and beryl. Lots of beryl. One beryl deposit filled three freight cars. Rock collectors will recognize more than 150 minerals in the walls of the caverns and tunnels.

For more information go to www.rugglesmine.com.

Santa's Village, Six Gun City, Story Land, and Adventure Suites

Santa's Village has a North Pole theme. Story Land is all about fairy tales and fantasy. Six Gun City features the rootin'-tootin' Wild West. All three have been in business for more than 50 years and are within spittin' distance of each other in Glen and Jefferson.

While you're right there, why not extend the experience with a stay at Adventure Suites in North Conway? Each suite has a theme. The Roman Spa has Roman pillars, a round bed and a 50-inch HDTV just like in Ancient Rome. The Log Cabin features a log fireplace run with gas, and wooden sculptures. The Cave includes a waterfall shower, bats, and dinosaur bones. Also available: Dragon's Lair, Motorcycle Madness, and the Love Shack, with appropriate accoutrements. (That's French for *stuff*.) The Tree House Suite boasts a swing, climbing wall, and a Jacuzzi.

Shaker Village and Enfield Shaker Museum

I can remember when the last of the Shakers, two elderly eldresses, were still in residence at Shaker Village on Shaker

Road in Canterbury. But they're long gone, buried in a cemetery without headstones—to make mowing easier. The Shakers were an amazing group, always thinking and inventing. What they didn't do was have sex or, consequently, children. Which accounts for the current shortage of Shakers.

Their legacy lives on. Shaker Village preserves 29 Shaker buildings and 694 acres of woods, fields, gardens, and millponds. The museum store sells Shaker reproductions and country goods, including the famous oval boxes and flat brooms. Shakers invented flat brooms.

Alan Shepard Jr. of Derry was the first American to travel through space, in his capsule, *Freedom 7*, he traveled about 300 miles in just over 15 minutes reaching a top speed of 5,180 miles an hour.

The Alan B. Shepard Discovery Center is the newest addition to the Christa McAuliffe Planetarium in Concord. Christa McAuliffe was America's first teacher in space. She didn't make it back, when the Space Shuttle *Challenger* crashed on January 28, 1986. That's a sad story.

Enfield Shaker Museum, Route 4-A, is not as big an operation, but it's home to the Great Stone Dwelling, which is very big and made of stone, the largest Shaker building in the country. When it was built it was the second most expensive building ever built in New Hampshire. Only the State House in Concord was more pricey. The Great Stone Dwelling looks just the same as it did when it was built more than 150 years ago. Those Shakers built to last. And they were good dancers, too. Enfield's website is www.shakermuseum.org.

Strawbery Banke

Sort of an Old Williamsburg North, Strawbery Banke in olde Portsmouth is a living museum of 30 olde houses and olde gardens in the olde Puddle Dock part of town, representing 400 years of colonial history. The reason *Strawbery Banke* is spelled funny is because it's spelled the olde way.

Cool places to shop (remember, no sales tax!)

Most people head straight for the outlets. For the Tilton outlets, scoot straight up 93 to exit 20 and you're there. Everything's cheaper than at the mall, if you're in the market for mall stuff. Among the outlets: Mesa, Coach, Lane Bryant, Eddie Bauer, Van Heusen, Jockey—everything from plates to underpants at a discount. It's a happy place. And no sales tax!

For the North Conway outlets, scoot straight up Route 16, hang a sharp left (still 16) in Conway, and you'll know you've arrived when you see stores to the left and stores to the right and lots of people walking around with glazed eyes carrying bags full of bargains. North Conway has more outlets than Tilton, over 60 at the Settlers' Green Outlet Village alone, but the driving is tougher. Route 16 in summer or foliage season can get busy. It's one of those keep-your-lights-on-during-the-day roads, i.e., hairy.

Calef's Country Store

For a more authentic New Hampshire shopping experience, I recommend Calef's Country Store in Barrington, run by my friends, Lindy and Cleve Horton. It's at the intersection of Routes 125 and 9 at Calef's Corner. Calef's, in business since

1869, prides itself on stocking stuff you can't get just anywhere, like old-fashioned snappy cheese, New Hampshire–made jellies and pickles, and Becky Rule humor CDs. You can get sandwiches, too. And next door there's a gift shop. Behind the deli counter you'll find the not-so-hidden treasure, Joel Sherburne, who's worked at Calef's since Christ wore knickers. He's the keeper of the cheese and the lore. And he likes to visit! Visit calefs.com for more information.

Tuttle's Red Barn

Talk about historic. Tuttle's farm on Dover Point Road in Dover is the oldest continuously working farm in the country. Dates back to 1632 when John Tuttle settled on a plot of land with nothing but an ax and two pewter candleholders. John's descendants, 12 generations later, sell replicas of those candleholders in Tuttle's Red Barn. They also sell fresh produce, an array of cheeses, and all kinds of gourmet (that means tasty and fancy) goodies. What was once a farmstand by the side of the road is now a 9,000-square-foot food and gift emporium. As is the case at Calef's, the locals shop Tuttle's just as much as the tourists, which is how you know it's good stuff at reasonable prices.

Tuttle's Red Barn: The Story of America's Oldest Family Farm tells the story generation by generation. Richard Michelson wrote it. Caldecott-winner Mary Azarian illustrated the book for kids. It's for sale at Tuttle's Red Barn, or www.tuttlesredbarn.net.

Antiques and secondhand shops

In this part of the country, we're loaded with old—old houses, old cemeteries, old churches, the oldest free public library in the country (Peterborough, 1833), old inns, old farts. Let me rephrase: We're blessed with historic houses, cemeteries, churches, libraries, inns, etc. Or, put another way, vintage. We've got antiques shops up the wazoo. We like antiques. We like having them in our homes, and when we get sick of them or hard up for cash, we especially enjoy selling them in yard sales to dealers who then sell them to tourists at a substantial markup. Never be afraid to say, "Could you do a little better?" That's N'Hampsha for "Reduce the price of Grammie's chamberpot from what's marked on the tag to what we really wanted it for in the first place." If we want $10, we put $15 on it, leaving plenty of room to dicka.

Antique Alley runs along Route 4, the Old New Hampshire Turnpike, from Epsom through Northwood, splattering over into Chichester in the west and Lee in the east. The Alley has the highest density of antiques and secondhand shops in the state, more than 50 dealers on a 20-mile stretch. Northwood has the highest concentration. I won't say every other house is an antiques shop, but pretty close.

If you like old stuff, plan to make a day of it. Catch lunch at Chadbourn's Restaurant, Johnson's Dairy Bar, the Northwood Diner—all on the main drag, all family-owned establishments. Or try Susty's Radical Vegan Cafe on the corner of Routes 4 and 43 if you like tofu and greens. Say hi to Norma. She's a peach.

8

Four-Season Activities (Native-style)

What do you do in New Hampshire all winter?
Wise-ass answer: Mostly we staht cahs.
What do you do in New Hampshire all summer?
Wise-ass answer: Summer?

Whether you visit in January or June, there's always something going on. Here are a few of the highlights. This is what we natives do, and you can, too—and should, if you want the REAL New Hampshire experience.

Winter

Ski

Me, I don't. I've tried. Took lessons as a kid. Most kids here do. The schools ship them to ski areas once a week or so during the winter so they'll learn. I just never got the hang of sliding down a steep hill on two sticks freezing my . . . feet off. Even the hot chocolate in the lodge burned my tongue. I do cross-country ski out back of the house, because that's like walking. Walking I can do.

That said, I've been told that New Hampshire is a skier's paradise. We got mountains. We got snow and the capacity to make snow if Old Man Winter gets stingy. We got lifts to take you up

139

the mountains so you don't have to walk. At www.skinh.com you can find out how much snow each ski area has, what the snow's like (crunchy, crusty, grainy, slushy, powdery, fluffy, icy, crispy, creamy), how many lifts are available, and lots more. The site even has a weekly "on snow" video, showing someone skiing, on the snow, at each ski area.

Besides downhill skiing, many of our ski resorts—from Attitash to Wildcat—have places for cross-country skiing, snow-boarding, and snow tubing. Many are even four-season resorts. Ragged Mountain in Danbury has a golf course. At Loon you can ride the gondola to the top year-round. Loon also hosts the Highland Games each September. Mount Sunapee offers sky rides to the top of the mountain on the chairlift and hosts the annual New Hampshire Craftsmen's Fair in August.

Skiing is big business in New Hampshire. So strap on those sticks, ride the chair to the top and go for it, but go careful. Try to stay upright. If you fall hard, you could break a bone. Then

In Woodford, Old Scooch wanted to get rid of his falling-down house since he'd put up a spanky new modular on the property. But he didn't want to pay to have it torn down or have the debris hauled away, and he wasn't able to do it himself on account of his sciatica. He offered the house to the fire department to do a practice burn. From time to time they'd burn a shack or an old barn to test their skills. They called it "a controlled burn," ran around with hoses, wore their helmets and fireproof suits.

But the chief turned him down. Didn't give a good reason. Just turned him down flat. Old Scooch was pissed off. Time passed. Scooch called the chief for a burn permit. He'd pruned the apple trees, piled the prunings up nice, and since it was a drizzly day, seemed like a good time to get rid of the unsightly pile. What he didn't tell the chief was that the unsightly pile was on the old porch.

the ski patrol has to haul you off
the mountain on a toboggan.

Burn brush

If there's snow on the ground
and it's after December, it's legal in
many towns to burn brush without
having to bother with a permit,
which can be a pain. You have to
call the volunteer fire chief, drive
out to his house, get him to sign a
paper that says you can only burn a
certain time on a certain day. By
the time you get all that done, you
don't feel like burning anymore.

All year long we pile brush—
branches we trimmed or that fell
in the driveway, bushes we cut, what's left of the trees we
yarded out for cordwood. Come some crisp, clear winter
evening, we scrape the snow away and burn the pile. Have to
start small, with dry pine needles, newspaper, and twigs. But
gradually you'll get some coals and pretty soon the whole
thing's blazing. Don't forget the hot dogs and marshmallows!

Lately towns have been tightening up on brush-burning regulations, but years ago we were pretty loose on the subject. A
woman from Tamworth said when she first moved to town
from the South (Long Island, I believe), she called the chief at
the all-volunteer fire department to inquire about torching a
pile left over from land clearing for her new house. "Do I need
a permit?" she asked.

"Nope."

New Hampshirite workout

- Haul your chain saw out to the wood lot and fell two big maples and a dead oak
- Limb them
- Pile the brush
- Cut up the big stuff
- Haul it out in a wheelbarrow—25 loads
- Split it
- Pile it
- Call it good

"What are the rules then?"

"No rules," he said. "But we'd appreciate it if you didn't burn until after six. We all work out of town and a lot of us don't get home 'til suppertime.

First Night

If you don't have a brush pile of your own, you can see stars, sparks, waterfalls and umbrellas at one of our First Nights, last day of December into the wee hours of January 1. Wolfeboro puts on a lively First Night complete with giant puppets in the parade and fireworks over Lake Winnipesaukee.

Portsmouth celebrates all over the city. Churches open their doors for music and the West End StudioTheatre stages a holiday-appropriate show like *It's a Wonderful Life*, with puppets. We love puppets. New Hampshire ranks highest in per capita puppeteers in New England. We rank second in clowns. Massachusetts has more. They elect them.

Other deep-winter activities

- Skate
- Sled
- Snowshoe
- Slog through slush
- Shovel roof
- Shovel driveway
- Shovel path to mulch pile and bird feeder
- Chop ice from steps
- Prune apple trees
- Braid rugs
- Peruse gardening catalogs
- Drink heavily

- Wonder why we don't live someplace warm, like Rhode Island
- Hibernate

And you might want to consider

The Northwood Crank Pullers Annual Radar Run and Dinner Dance

This dance is held toward the end of January at Lake Shore Farm. Go to the www.northwoodcrankpullers.com for details. Other snow sled clubs around the state hold similar events in which snowmobiles race against the clock or each other on glare ice. In the Crank Pullers event, antique snowmobiles, 25 years or older, race for free.

Ice fishing is a popular winter sport. A fella from Massachusetts wanted to try his hand at it. "Go out in the the middle of the cove," the native advised. "Cut a hole and go to it." The next day, the native asked the fella from away how the fishing went. "Geez," the fella said, "by the time I cut a hole big enough for the boat, I was too tired to fish."

We used to have water-ride fund-raisers where snowmobiles would get going real fast on the ice, then try to jump or skim an expanse of open water. Small wagers were placed. The water wouldn't be deep enough to drown anybody if they didn't quite make it. And organizers always had ropes and burly men on hand to pull out the machine and rider. But the Legislature spoiled our fun and made water rides illegal. Next thing you know they'll outlaw Cow Pie Bingo or Roadkill Rummy.

The Penguin Plunge

The Penguin Plunge at Hampton Beach raises money for Special Olympics of New Hampshire. Generally held on Super Bowl Sunday, who needs football when you can run into the Atlantic in your Speedo.

If you don't want to commit to the plunge, stand back, shivering, and watch, dressed in your chicken suit. Live music provided and lots of good eats.

The Colebrook Winter Carnival

This carnival in early February features a Little Jack Frost and Snowflake Pageant, as well as ice carving, bocce ball (like bowling without alleys or pins), and cribbage tournaments. If there's enough snow, which there usually is, there are snowshoe relays and dogsled races.

The Great Rotary Fishing Derby

The Derby in Meredith takes place each February and attracts hundreds of optimists who drill holes and drop a line. Somtimes they jig. Sometimes they sits and thinks. Sometimes they just sits. Catch the biggest fish and win a new truck.

Spring

- Rake the yard for what you missed last fall and what the dogs left this winter
- Cut up the limbs that broke off and the trees that keeled over during winter, keeping a close eye out for poison ivy, which is cspecially potent in May
- Plant peas as soon as the ground gets soft
- Wash windows

144

- Beat and air out rugs
- Complain about the mud
- Dig holes while the ground is soft
- Collect rocks while the ground is soft to add to the wall
- Go fishing on opening day if you can find a parking place
- Cut pussy willows
- Count lady's slippers
- Get the cat spayed
- Give the dog a bath
- Remember how bad the blackflies are because they're BAACK
- Curse the blackflies
- Smell the lilacs (especially if you're in Dover, the Lilac City)

Wear your cup on your head

An old New Hampshire remedy for escaping pesky hoss- and deerflies—the big ones that really hurt when they bite—is simple and sort of secret. But I'll let you in on it because I like you.

Get a hat. A baseball cap, fishing hat, straw hat, whatever you like. Glue a blue or yellow (these are the only colors that work) cup to the top of it. Paint the rest of it, inside and out, with stickum or stickum substitute—anything that stays sticky for a long time. Honey mixed with a little water works fine.

Put the hat on your head and you're good to go. Instead of getting in your face, those hoss- and deerflies will fly into the stickum and get stuck. End of problem.

And nobody will laugh at the blue or yellow cup on your head.

Trust me.

And you might want to consider

Blessing of the Bikes

This annual and popular event draws bikers from all over the country and takes place the weekend after Father's Day in Colebrook at the Shrine of Our Lady of Grace on Route 3 just south of town. We're not talking bicycles, we're talking BIKES.

145

Motorcycles. Suzukis, Kawasakis, Indians, Hondas, Husqvarnas, Viagras, and Harleys. Especially Harleys. Vaaarooom-rooom-roooom. They roar in by the hundreds, causing the moose to look at one another, puzzled, and say: "What the heck?" Causing the locals to flee. And, they fill every inn, hotel, and campground in a fifty-mile radius.

Actually, you can get anything with wheels or bogies blessed at the Blessing of the Bikes, from RVs to snowmachines. It's a big loud party, Friday through Sunday, complete with commemorative T-shirts and hats, a bike rodeo, prizes for "Best Most Original; Best Customized; Best Overall," a parade, and "The Great North Woods Ride-in."

Summer

- Mow lawns
- Drink iced tea with lemon
- Swat mosquitoes
- Curse mosquitoes
- Read books by New Hampshire writers like me
- Boat
- Lay out in the sun and tan up
- Climb mountains (you can climb a mountain anytime, but in summer you'll have more company and less chance of frostbite)
- Watch the Manchester Fisher Cats play baseball (our very own Double-A team)
- Vacation in Maine (if you're a local)
- Ooh and ahh over Fourth of July fireworks
- Cook lots of meat outdoors
- Go to the fair

Make your own moose-turd beads

Moose droppings make lovely jewelry when properly dried and varnished. To go green, go brown. Impress your friends with genuine New Hampshire moose-dropping earrings, necklaces, bracelets, tie tacks, tongue studs. Available at upscale gift shops thoughout the state.

Or, you can make your own. When moose go, they leave a pile. One pile might contain as many as 200 individual turds. Make sure the pile is fresh and the turds are still soft. Scoop them up in a plastic bag. Once you get them home, follow this six-step process:

1) Lay the turds out on waxed paper on a cookie sheet, no turd touching another (so they won't stick together).

2) With a toothpick, large needle, ice pick or other thin, sharp instrument, make a hole in each turd for stringing later.

3) Put the turds in a warm dry place until they have dried and hardened. This could take a week or two.

4) Once they are hard and dry, finish them off with a clear lacquer, available at crafts or home improvement stores. The more coats of lacquer applied, the shinier the bead. Be sure to let the lacquer dry after each coat. Be careful not to fill the beading holes with lacquer. Best to poke your sharp instrument through each hole after each application of lacquer. (Some people paint their turds different colors. Others prefer the natural mahogany brown.)

5) Once your turds have reached the desired level of shine, you're ready to string them. Incorporate them in earrings, bracelets, necklaces, headbands, as you would any high-quality bead. Monofilament fish line works great for necklaces, but any strong thin thread will do. Clasps, earring mounts, etc., available at crafts stores.

6) Enjoy.

The agricultural fair season begins in late July with the North Haverhill Fair and ends in October with the Sandwich Fair. The highlight of each fair is, of course, the animals—pigs, cows, sheep, goats, poultry, horses. Don't miss the tractor-, ox-, and horse-pulling contests. Most have midways. Some have gambling. Entertainment can range from a magic show to a country singer who you might have heard of. All serve tasty food from funnel cakes to sausages. Admission is reasonable. For most fairs you get a rake-off if you buy your tickets in advance.

NH fair schedule

Not set in stone, but this is generally how it goes:

July	North Haverhill Fair
	Stratham Fair
July	Cheshire Fair
August	Cornish Fair
August	Lancaster Fair
	Hopkinton Fair
September	Rochester Fair
September	Deerfield Fair
October	Sandwich Fair

And you might want to consider

Market Square Day

For the last thirty years, on the second Saturday in June, the streets of downtown Portsmouth are closed to cars for a giant block party. Sidewalks are lined with booths—things to buy, things to learn about, organizations to join. Music fills the air. There is dancing! Highlights: 10K Road Race, pancake breakfast, clambake, and lots of entertainment. An estimated 60,000 people descended on downtown for Market Square Day 2007. That's more than twice the population of the city.

The only thing that can dampen Market Square Day is torrential rain. It happens. When it does, head to Molly Malone's for a beer and a bowl of mulligan stew, or the nearest cafe for a cappuccino and a brioche. If you order cappuccino and brioche, you get coffee and a bun, plus the thrill of saying, "Uno cappuccino and uno brioche, see voo play." People will think you speak Italian and French.

The League of New Hampshire Craftsmen's Fair

This annual fair takes place in early August in Sunapee. It's among the oldest crafts fairs in the country. The first was held in Crawford Notch in 1933. The fair moved around the state some after that, before settling at the Mount Sunapee Ski Resort in 1964. More than 200 booths feature all kinds of handmade goods—wooden lampshades, felted

Delphine Aube once won second place in the horse-pulling contest at the North Haverhill Fair. He even got a trophy. Whenever company would come, Del would get out his trophy and tell the story of how he won second place in the horse-pulling contest at the North Haverhill Fair. Until one day, he went to get the trophy and it wasn't where he thought it would be. Maybe it was in the attic? Or the cellar? Or tucked into a closet?

Years passed. The trophy never turned up, and Delphine got out of the habit of telling the story of how he won second place in the horse-pulling contest.

After he died, his sons were pulling down an old shed on the property—previously an outhouse. They got the building down and were digging around with a shovel, when *clink clink*. The blade of the shovel struck something metal. Sure enough, it was Del's trophy.

They took the trophy to the house. "Look, Mother," they said, holding the trophy aloft.

"Oh," she said. "You found it."

149

hats, patchwork jackets, moose jewelry, pots, bowls made from burls, stained-glass dragons. All kinds of good stuff that you didn't know you needed, but once you see it, you realize you can't go home without it. Bring your pocketbook! Support our local artisans.

Old Home Day

Our beloved Old Home Day tradition can be traced to our beloved Governor Frank Rollins, who wrote: "Come back, come back! Do you not hear the call? What has become of the old home where you were born?"

He went on to talk about our rolling hills, rambling farmhouses, fragrant lilacs, shimmering poplars, weeping willows. In 1899, he declared an official Old Home Week, a time for those who'd moved away to return for a visit. A lot of towns still celebrate, including Boscawen, Salisbury, Candia, and South Sutton. Typically, there are parades, ham and bean suppers, maybe an auction or flea market, a cow-pie-throwing contest, a band in the gazebo, various exciting activities. In South Sutton folks dress in vintage clothes for the celebration. Any vintage will do, which makes for a nifty mix: Pilgrim, Colonial, Victorian. Put on an old hat and a shawl, you're good to go.

Fall

Leaf peeping

We all do it. The range of foliage color in New Hampshire is a wide one because of our mix of hardwoods. Birch can turn canary yellow, sugar maple cherry red. Some years are better than others. But if we get a good cold snap to remind the trees to change over and not too much hard rain to take the leaves down prematurely, the brilliance of the foliage can make even a native shift the wood splitter into neutral and say of the sugar maple in his own yard: "Ain't that pretty."

Deer hunters say, "Did you get your deer?" as though for each hunter there is one deer with his or her name on it waiting to be bagged. Todd asked his buddy Smokey, "Did you get your deer this year, Smoke?"

Smokey said: "We got pretty well skunked. Nobody in the family got a deer . . . except for Mother."

"What did she get him with?"

"The Buick."

Fall somehow surprises us every time with its color and mild weather, even those of use who've lived here all our lives (so far).

A friend told me a plan for retirement: Start in the north and follow the foliage south as the cold sets in and the leaves gradually change. Follow the foliage all the way down the coast and stretch out the season. Do they have foliage in Florida? What about Connecticut? I'm just wondering how far he'd get before he ran out.

Stack wood

November is the month when it finally sinks in that winter will come again and we're probably going to live to see it. Therefore, we better get the wood put up. Whether we yarded it off our own land or bought six cords of 16-inch dry off a guy from Pittsfield, that wood ain't going to stack itself. In less civilized places, maybe people would just leave it in a pile just the way it slid off the dump truck. But here we take pride in our woodpiles. A tidy woodpile is a work of art (pronounced *aht*).

They say wood warms you twice—when you haul it and when you burn it. But lucky ones get warmed seven times—in the felling, the trimming, the cutting to length, the hauling out of the woods, the splitting, the stacking, and, then, the burning. We like to think of wood work as New Hampshire aerobics. It's why we're all so buff under our five layers of clothes.

And you might want to consider

The Highland Games

Held over a three-day weekend late in September, the Highland Games at Loon Mountain fill every parking place in the town of Lincoln. You'll park at a school or a business lot and be bused to the mountain. This is the largest celebration of all things Scottish in New England. Men in kilts—everywhere! Even the Lincoln police officers, who provide security at the games, dress in kilts. You never saw so many knobby knees in your life. Music and dancing—world-class and constant at several venues on the site, including the New England Regional Scottish Fiddle Championship and the National Highland Dance Competition. Heavyweight Scottish athletics features burly men (in kilts), throwing weighty objects great distances. At the sheepdog trials—my favorite—the border collies run on the ski trail so you can see their every move. Many vendors. Tents for each clan where you can schmooze with your relatives or those you suspect might be. Oh, and did I mention bagpipes? Haggis? Whiskey tasting?

I go every year. It's grand!

The Winchester Pickle Festival

Not far from Keene in the small town of Winchester, the fourth Saturday in September (usually) is the date of the Pickle Festival. On Friday night, the festivities kick off with fireworks. On Saturday there's a parade, with marching pickles, lots of booths at town center selling pickles and pickle-related para-phernalia, like pickle earrings and refrigerator magnets. The pickles are in jars or barrels, some served on sticks. Flavors include dill, mustard, sour, garlic, and peppered. Other pickled foods also available. As it turns out, most anything can be pickled. Let your taste buds be your guide. Plenty of music and frivolity. You'll be tickled by the pickles.

The Giant Pumpkin Weigh-Off and Regatta

This extravaganza takes place in mid-October in Goffstown, pretty nearly ever year. One year it had to be canceled because of heavy rain, but that was a fluke. Typically, the Friday-through-Sunday events include a barn dance, dog costume contest, barbecue, police dog demonstration, pie-eating contest, pumpkin catapulting, great pumpkin shopping cart race, and pumpkin bowling. In the mini-pumpkin race, 500 gourds float down the river fast as they can.

Highlights: the weighing of the pumpkins and, of course, the regatta of giant pumpkin boats on the Piscataquog. People ride in these pumpkin boats. Pumpkins float, but they can be a dite unstable.

The Keene Pumpkin Festival

Held at the end of October, the "widest main street in the world" (this is true) is filled with 30,000 pumpkins, give or take, and even more people. As I write this, Boston holds the record for 30,128 pumpkins in one place—that record set in 2006. But it's just a matter of time before Keene regains top position. Those people are inspired when it comes to pumpkins.

The first festival in 1991 attracted just 600 pumpkins. Word got out that the festival was the place to be if you're a pumpkin,

How to Play FARKLE

If you're here on vacation and want a fun way to pass long evenings in your lavishly appointed room at the Balsams Grand Hotel or rainy days in the RV at Wallis Sands, try FARKLE.

Each player has five dice in a lucky color of choice. If you have only one set of five dice, you can pass them around, but it's more fun and the game moves faster if everybody has their own. Also, if somebody has a cold, you won't be so apt to pass on the germs.

To start, each player rolls one die to see who goes first. High number wins.

FARKLE is played in rounds. At the beginning of each round, the player throws five dice. If no dice score—that is, if there are no 1s, 5s, or three-of-a-kind—everyone shouts FARKLE and the unlucky player gets an F. Next time, it's an A, and so forth. If you FARKLE five times, spelling FARKLE (like playing PIG in basketball), you're out of the game, reduced to eating cheese puffs and sipping a glass of elderberry mead from New Hampshire's own Piscassic Pond Winery, while the others play on.

If any dice score, you may throw again, setting aside at least one scoring die. But, if the next throw turns up no new 1s, 5s, or three-of-a-kind, you lose everything earned to that point in this turn. Early in the game, players must keep going until they accumulate 1,000 points in a round. This puts them on the board. It's possible to play the whole game, never get 1,000 points in a single turn, and never get on the board. This is frustrating. Luckily, it doesn't happen very often. After that first thousand, you can accumulate as few or as many points as you dare in a turn, realizing that if you keep rolling, and get no new 1's, 5's or three-of-a-kinds, you're done for that round with no score. If you've set aside all five dice for scoring, then you can throw them all again. Your turn ends when you say, "Enough," and record your score, or when the dice let you down, and you turn up no new score. Knowing when to stop pushing your luck is key in FARKLE. And in life.

How to score a roll

Single 1 = 100
Single 5 = 50
Three 1s = 1,000
Three-of-a-kind = the number X 100 (three 2s = 200; three 4s equals 400, etc.)
Four-of-a-kind = the value of the three-of-a-kind doubled (four 2s equals 200 X 2 or 400, four 4s equals 400 X 2 or 800, etc.)
Five-of-a-kind = the value of three-of-a-kind doubled and doubled again (five 2s equals 200 X 2 X 2 or 800, five 4s equals 400 X 2 X 2 or 1,600, etc.)
Straight, aka One-Shot Biggie (1-2-3-4-5 or 2-3-4-5-6) = 1,000
These scores are for a single throw. If you come up with three 1s in one roll, that's 1,000. But if you come up with three 1s in three rolls (setting aside one each time), that's 300. When a player gets 10,000 points, everyone else takes just one more turn to try to catch or pass that leader.

Hints: Throw at least three dice whenever you can. If this means setting aside the 1 from your first throw and re-throwing the 5 (which you could have set aside), that's fine. When you throw at least three dice, you have a chance at a three-of-a-kind.
Some dice are luckier than others. You may have to buy several sets to find your lucky five.

so the numbers have risen every year. Oh, and they're all lit! Check out the jack-o'-lantern photos at www.pumpkinfestival.com.

No wonder the pumpkin is New Hampshire's state fruit. Apples, eat your heart out.

9

Ghosts, Bigfoot, and Other Less Mainstream Attractions

This is all true. Really. We in New Hampshire are used to our ghosts, Bigfoots and UFOs, and darn proud of them. The less fainthearted of you tourists would be wise to seek out these attractions. Then you'd really have something to write on the postcards you send back to Ohio, Kansas, or wherever you hail from.

Why are they still hanging around?

Who? The Blue Lady

Where?

Vale End Cemetery in Wilton.

What's the problem?

Mary Ritter Spaulding seemed like a nice-enough person. She attended church, grew healing herbs, seemed content in her marriage, bore several children, and died a natural death in 1808. Still, she occasionally rises from her grave as a column of blue light. At night. Especially when it's foggy. (Maybe her rheumatiz acts up.) She does no harm, except scare the pants off locals. Though one wonders what the locals are doing in the cemetery on dark, foggy nights.

Who? The Disgruntled Voter

Where?

Alton Town Hall.

What's the problem?

Spotted from time to time by town employees, this ghost drops in on selectmen's meetings, walks the halls at night, floats in and out of rooms. Some see him. Some don't. Some hear his footsteps. Some notice doors opening on their own. Some hear voices when the building is empty. What's the Disgruntled Voter's gripe? My guess? Taxes.

Who? Madame Sherri

Where?

The burned-out remains of her "castle" in Chesterfield.

What's the Problem?

Was she a Bohemian, a flapper girl, or, perhaps, a madam? The vibrant Antoinette Sherri spent summers in Chesterfield beginning in the 1920s. She had a big car, a Packard, loads of money, and lots of exotic friends, including a bevy of young women who spent time at the big stone house she built on Gulf Road. The castle burned in the early sixties, leaving just the cellar hole, a fireplace, and the stone stairs.

This is weird: Madame Sherri died in 1965 at a nearby nursing home on the same day her property was sold. Evidently, she didn't approve of the sale. She haunts the place, floating about in her Roaring Twenties finery. Some who lay hands on the stone stairs can hear music playing as though Sherri and her friends are still living it up.

The nearly 500 acres are open to the public, owned now by the Society for the Preservation of New Hampshire Forests.

Who? Ocean-Born Mary

Where?

The Ocean-Born Mary House in Henniker.

What's the problem?

Pirate Don Pedro buried treasure on the premises and got himself murdered with a cutlass. According to the story, Mary, born at sea where she first met Don Pedro, found him and buried his body under a stone slab in the kitchen. Don Pedro is said to haunt the premises, perhaps protecting his treasure, or maybe pissed off that his murderer was never caught.

Or, is this a hoax cooked up by owners in the early 1900s, just for the heck of it?

Nah. Parapsychologists get woozy and tingly all over when they walk the halls of the Ocean-Born Mary house.

Current owners don't buy the ghost story and discourage visitors. But the Henniker Historical Society Museum displays a piece of the green silk dress Mary wore on the day she married James Wallace in 1742.

Old Rob's wife Clara finally succumbed. Though they lived in Strafford, Clara's family owned a plot in East Northwood, which is where she was laid to rest. After the funeral, Old Rob's friend Angus accompanied Old Rob on the long ride back to the empty farmhouse.

"You know," Old Rob said, "she was a fine woman. She was a wonderful wife to me for fifty-seven years. She did a wonderful job of raising our seven children, kept them clean and fed and towing the line. She was a wonderful housekeeper, too. And she could cook, my god, couldn't she cook. Her pies were the talk of the church suppers. A strong woman, she could hay as well as any man. She was a wonderful help with the farm work."

"Yup," Angus said. "Clara was a wonderful woman."

"You know," Old Rob said, "I never really liked her."

Haunted inns

According to our exhaustive research, just about every inn in New Hampshire sports a ghost or two. Some are more haunted than others. You might have to pay extra for the rooms where the bed shakes, the footsteps sound the loudest, and the moans, shrieks and whisperings are more likely to occur. But it's worth it. When you call to make a reservation, just ask if the inn is haunted and by whom.

Angel of the Mountains B&B, Bethlehem

A girl in red roams the halls looking for her lost love. She never finds him. Because she's DEAD.

Inn at Jackson

Haunted by a carpenter. The hammering and cursing sometimes wakes the guests.

Mount Washington Hotel, Bretton Woods

Carolyn Stickney, the original owner, spends most of her time haunting the tower rooms. She stares through windows. And changes TV stations. Evidently, she enjoys *American Idol*, *Ghost Whisperer*, and the Celtics.

Notchland Inn, Hart's Location

One clue to the haunting is the tombstone in the parlor that reads:

1778

NANCY BARTON

DIED IN A SNOWSTORM IN PURSUIT OF HER FAITHLESS LOVER

Nearby Nancy Pond is named for her.

Sise Inn, Portsmouth

The ghosts lock and unlock doors. They sometimes dub around with the ice machine on the third floor.

Sugar Hill Inn, Franconia

There's a man in the kitchen—but he's not doing any cooking.

Three Chimneys Inn, Durham

Haunted by a mischievious little girl who messes with computers, makes numbers appear backwards on calculators, sometimes throws glasses, and rearranges the furniture.

Mr. Bigfoot

Many people claim to have seen Bigfoots in New Hampshire, but it is my belief they're actually seeing sidehill wampuses. Basically, a sidehill wampus is a Bigfoot with one leg several inches shorter than the other. They stand about seven feet tall, go 300 to 400 pounds. The short leg lets them move easily around sidehills—long leg downhill, short leg uphill, evening things out—which is why they like drumlins. Get them on the flat, though, they limp like crazy.

We do have Bigfoots, but they're rare. And fast. Rarer still, eastern mountain lions. Only about a hundred people a year claim to see mountain lions—and nobody believes them, least of all the biologists at Fish and Game, whose standard line has long been: "There have been no mountain lions in New Hampshire since the 1800s."

They used to say the same thing about Bigfoots and wampuses.

Betty, Barney and the UFOs

This is a true story. Really! On September 19, 1961, near the Indian Head rock formation (looks like the head of an Indian in profile) in Lincoln, Betty and Barney Hill, aged 39 and 41, respectively, had a close encounter of the abductee kind. Just an ordinary couple from Portsmouth—he worked for the post office, she was a social worker—they were traveling home from a vacation in Montreal. It was a long ride to begin with, but the two hours they lost being inspected by aliens inside the UFO made it seem even longer.

The events unfolded something like this:

Late supper in Colebrook 10:05 PM. Back on the road, near Lancaster the couple spots a UFO. They lose sight of it behind Cannon Mountain. Near Indian Head the UFO hovers over them and crosses the road. Barney pulls over, gets out, and checks out the blinking, glowing sphere through handy binoculars. He sees some aliens in the windows. This upsets him, so he hops back in the car and speeds away to the sound of mysterious beeping. A while later, he drives off the main road and ends up at a roadblock—several aliens blocking the road. He stops. The UFO has landed nearby. Betty and Barney are taken inside and examined—scraped, poked, and prodded by little guys with big eyes. Later, they find themselves back on Route 3, headed south. A sign reads CONCORD 17 MILES.

They arrive home in Portsmouth after 5:00 AM.

Betty and Barney didn't want to talk about what had happened at first. Didn't remember what happened for a while. But gradually the story leaked and made a big ripple in the world of UFOlogy. The Hills got interrogated, hypnotized, and analyzed. Betty remembered that the aliens asked her why

162

Barney's teeth could be pulled out of his mouth, but hers couldn't. She tried her best to explain the concept of dentures. The aliens didn't get it.

Barney contracted a mysterious case of genital warts. Betty joined a network of believers and started seeing UFOs all over the place. In later years, she led expeditions to a secret landing site, said to be in Kingston, where people saw UFOs coming and going on a regular basis.

Their story spawned a book, *The Interrupted Journey* by John Fuller, published in 1966, and a TV movie, *The UFO Incident*, starring James Earl Jones and Estelle Parsons. The Hillses' tale is also the source of much of what we know about UFOs and the aliens who pilot them. The Hills were the first to recall details like anal probes, skin scrapings, and big needles in the abdomen to test for pregnancy. Elements such as missing time, induced memory loss, telepathic communication, wraparound eyes, and star

The Betty and Barney Hill UFO Tour

You people from away can retrace the drive Betty and Barney took the night they were abducted. Start in Colebrook. Head south on Route 3. They spotted the UFO in Lancaster, so look sharp. Drive on through Twin Mountain. Pass Cannon where they lost sight of the the huge glowing sphere when it ducked behind the mountain.

When you see road signs for Indian Head, you're close to where Betty and Barney had their close encounter. In North Woodstock slide off Route 3 onto 175 and keep going to Plymouth, where you can pick up Route 3 again. Catch 93 in Concord and head east to Portsmouth.

It took seven hours for the Hills to make the trip that, some say, should have taken around five, leaving approximately two hours for the abduction.

If it takes you more than seven hours, consider hypnosis.

163

maps showing where the aliens hailed from—now staples of
the UFO canon—were new when the Hills first told their
story. Without Betty and Barney we might not have had *Close
Encounters of the Third Kind* or *The X-Files*.

The whole matter is poked, probed and analyzed in
*Encounters at Indian Head: The Betty and Barney Hill UFO Abduction
Revisited*. In 2000, editors Karl Pflock and Peter Brookesmith
and other UFOlogists, philosophers, and debunkers, along with
Betty Hill herself, returned to the scene of the mystery for a
symposium. Their book, a thorough examination of the subject,
came out in 2007. One photo in *Encounters* shows the whole
gang on the side of the road near the clearing where the UFO
landed. The caption explains how a local in a passing pickup
truck pulled over and called out, "Did ya see a moose?"

"Nope," the researchers replied. "Looking for UFOs."

UFOs in Exeter and other hot spots

In the sixties a common pastime in New Hampshire was
UFO spotting. We'd camp out at night in a field or by a lake
with a good view of the sky and wait for the UFOs to come
along. They often did, though they usually moved fast and kept
their distance so it was hard to get a good photograph.

In 1965, a large one hovered over Exeter long enough for a
hitchhiking teenager to dive into a ditch, terrified. Afterwards,
the thing still hovering, he sneaked away and caught a ride to
the police station, where his obvious terror and disheveled
appearance seemed to support his tale. Two officers went to
the scene, where they too saw the object, big as a house with
blinking red lights, before it flew silently away.

164

This caused quite a stir in town. Several others came forward to report sightings of the mysterious object. They've been seeing UFOs in Exeter and surrounds ever since.

Fifty miles north in Wakefield, something crashed through the ice on a farm pond in the middle of the winter, causing men in suits from Washington to come to the farm, stand around the pond, and look at the hole. It was a big, round hole.

Come spring they dredged the pond, but didn't find a spaceship. I believe all they came up with was the rusted carcass of an old truck. What caused the big round hole in the ice of that farm pond remains a touchy subject around town. Some say UFO; some say no. If you have lunch at the Miss Wakefield Diner or the Poor People's Pub, both fine eateries, I wouldn't bring it up.

You don't hear as much about UFOs these days as you used to. But doing in-depth research for this book, I discovered, sure enough, they continue to come around, ignored by media too concerned with misbehaving Hollywood starlets to notice vehicles from other galaxies. According to the NUFORC (National UFO Reporting Center), UFOs have been sighted in Londonderry, Franconia Notch, Bethlehem, Contoocook, Alton, Raymond, Eaton, Warner, Whitefield, Littleton, Meredith, Success, Salisbury, South Kingston, New Ipswich, Hanover, Kensington, Raymond, Durham, Laconia, Exeter, and Lisbon—and that's just in 2007. Heck, I'm looking at one in my backyard right now. It's landed on the septic mound we call "Thunder Mountain." I can see it clearly. But that's not the scary part. The scary part is that one googly eye on the side of the little gray fella's head staring back at me through the windshield.

Time for another beer.

10

Quiz Time

1) In New Hampshire it's illegal to
   (a) ride a motorcycle without a helmet
   (b) ride in a car without fastening your seat belt
   (c) buy fireworks
   (d) none of the above

2) What is Manchester's main street, Elm Street, famous for?
   (a) It is paved with granite
   (b) It dead-ends in both directions
   (c) George Washington once slept there
   (d) It is the widest main street in America

3) What was the first city in the state to get streetlights?
   (a) Nashua
   (b) Woodsville
   (c) Berlin
   (d) Portsmouth

4) Who was Bill Loeb?
   (a) The outspoken ultraconservative publisher of the *Manchester Union Leader*, who famously said: "Things are either right or they are wrong."
   (b) A catcher for the Red Sox in the 1970s

(c) A famous heart surgeon from Deering who invented shunts

(d) Nackey Loeb's husband

5) Who's Pudge Fisk?

(a) A catcher for the Red Sox in the 1960s and a native of Charlestown

(b) The first governor of New Hampshire

(c) My great-uncle

(d) Inventor of the Old Man of the Mountain Bobblehead

6) What's a fisher cat?

(a) A house cat with scaly markings and a taste for tuna

(b) A wild cat that catches and eats salmon

(c) A small wolverine

(d) A baseball player

7) Which of the following is *not* a town in New Hampshire?

(a) Goshen

(b) Bethlehem

(c) Jerusalem

(d) Alexandria

8) When a native says, "Let's slide down to Newick's and shoot the wad," what is she suggesting?

(a) Target practice in the sandpit

(b) Shopping for shoes

(c) White-water rafting on the Newick River

(d) Ordering the fisherman's platter at Newick's Seafood Restaurant

9) "Live Free or Die" is:

(a) A flavor of Stonyfield yogurt—prune, oatmeal, and a touch of castor oil

(b) A rock band

(c) Our state motto

(d) Our state song, written by Steve Tyler of Aerosmith

10) Where are the Polar Caves?

(a) The Arctic

(b) The Antarctic

(c) Plymouth

(d) On the side of Polar Mountain

Answers

1) (d) In the Live Free or Die State, you are free to ride a motorcycle with the wind blowing through your hair. You are also free—if you're an adult—to ride in a car without a seat belt. We're the only state in the union without a mandatory seat-belt law for adults.

You're also free to buy all the fireworks you want. (No sales tax!) You just can't set the fireworks off. That is illegal, with a few exceptions like small sparklers and Roman candles. So buy all the Bottle Rockets, Sky Flyers, Exploding Snakes, and Mega-Wheelies you want, but don't touch them off until you've crossed a couple of state lines. All of the above are forbidden in Maine, Massachusetts, and Vermont, too. And yet, Phantom Fireworks of Seabrook has the largest fireworks showroom in New England. Of course, if you've got a permit, you're all set.

2) (b) Elm Street dead-ends twice.

3) (c) In 1877 fourteen electric streetlights were installed on Main Street in Berlin, the first in New Hampshire. At that time Berlin was a booming mill town and one of the richest and most progressive cities in New England.

4) (a & d) Bill Loeb published the *Union Leader* for more than 30 years. He was also married to Nackey Scripps Loeb, the granddaughter of E.W. Scripps, newspaper tycoon. Known for his far-right Republican politics and scathing editorials, he called Harry Truman incompetent, Dwight Eisenhower a hypocrite, and JFK a liar. During the 1972 campaign he wrote an editorial so harsh it made Ed Muskie cry, ending the Mainer's presidential bid. In 1975 Kevin Cash published *Who the Hell IS William Loeb?*, an unauthorized biography of the man some called "the meanest S.O.B. in New Hampshire."

5) (a) Carlton "Pudge" Fisk played ball at the University of New Hampshire. As a professional, he holds the record for catching more games than any other player and hitting more home runs than any other catcher. In 1975 Pudge played a key role in the 1975 World Series, which the goddamn Red Sox almost won.

6) (c & d) A fisher cat is the big brother of the marten and the little brother of the wolverine. It doesn't catch fish and it's not a cat. They're fast and ferocious, enjoying a diet of squirrels, mice, porcupines, and house cats. The Fisher Cats are also the Manchester-based Double-A affiliate of the Toronto Blue Jays.

7) (c) Biblical and historical as they sound, Goshen, Bethlehem, and Alexandria are all small towns in New Hampshire. Jerusalem's in Israel.

Bethlehem, population 2,200, has a large Jewish population and a synagogue that serves much of the North Country. At Christmas, the post office gets extra busy with folks wanting their Christmas cards postmarked Bethlehem.

8) (d) Newick's Seafood Restaurant in Newington serves heaps of fried fish at a reasonable price, so when you "shoot the wad" and go all out for the big one, the fisherman's platter, you won't break the bank. In business since 1948, it started as a roadside stand run by a lobstering family. Recently, Newick's has also opened restaurants in Concord and Dover.

9) (c) It's our state motto. What does it mean, exactly? Your guess is as good as mine.

10) (c) The Polar Caves, a tourist attraction in Plymouth on Route 25, are cavities among massive rock slabs piled up by the glaciers. You can climb on to the Raven's Roost, walk among them on the boardwalk, or squirm through the Lemon Squeeze.

If you answered:

All 10 questions correctly: You must be a native!

7 to 9 correctly: You've either been studying up or you've been here so long we're beginning to get used to you.

4 to 6 correctly: You're either a good guesser or you've been around long enough to pick up the basics.

Just 1 correct answer: Welcome to New Hampshire.

No correct answers? Well, now you know.

Where Would You Find . . . ?

(1) Jacob's Ladder
  (a) On the side of Mount Washington
  (b) In the herb garden
  (c) Right next to Jacob's step stool
  (d) All of the above

(2) The Imp
  (a) The State House
  (b) Museum of Childhood, Wakefield
  (c) Pinkham Notch
  (d) All of the above

(3) Pig With Snout
  (a) The Currier Museum of Art
  (b) On the menu at the Road Kill Cafe
  (c) At Charmingfare Farm in Candia
  (d) All of the above

(4) The worst weather in the world
  (a) The Isles of Shoals
  (b) The moon
  (c) The top of Mount Washington
  (d) All of the above

(5) The most unusual place Alan Shepard Jr. ever played golf
  (a) The highlands of Scotland
  (b) Beaver Meadow Golf Club in Concord
  (c) Peak of Mount Monadnock
  (d) The moon

Answers

(1) (d) Jacob's Ladder is the steepest part of the 3 ¼-mile ride up Mount Washington on the Cog Railway. The maximum gradient on the 25-foot trestle is over 37 percent, i.e., very steep. I'd explain what *maximum gradient* means, but that would involve algebra. I don't do algebra.

Jacob's Ladder is also an herb with blue flowers and delicate paired leaves that grows between 1 and 3 feet high. It's used in the treatment of headaches, trembling, heart palpitations, and nervous complaints, such as those experienced by riders of the Cog as they make the harrowing climb up Jacob's Ladder.

Jacob's ladder can also be found in Nick Penny's garage, right next to his step stool.

(2) (c) The Imp, a stone profile, can be seen from the Dolly Copp Road in Pinkham Notch. You can climb the Imp Trail up Imp Mountain for a closer look.

The Museum of Childhood in Wakefield has many dolls, old and new, but no imps to my knowledge.

The State House is the workplace of legislators, the Governor's Council, the governor, the secretary of state, and other politicos. If there are imps among them, they have not come out of the closet— although I do know of at least one Democratic leprechaun, a Republican pixie, and two Libertarian gnomes.

(3) (a) Pig With Snout is a charcoal drawing by Maud Morgan, circa 1939–1940 from the collection at the Currier Museum of Art in Manchester.

(4) (c) The consensus among weather watchers is that the worst weather in the world occurs on Mount Washington, a combination of wind, snow, and cold. If your answer was the moon, I fooled you. The moon is out of this world.

(5) (d) Astronaut Alan Shepard Jr., the fifth man to walk on the moon, couldn't resist driving a couple of balls while he was right there.

11

Good-bye

You are now leaving New Hampshire. Please come back soon.

I hope the information on these pages doesn't lead you too far astray. Hope you don't end up in Claremont when you were trying to get to Keene. Hope the wild boars leave you be and the aliens keep their distance. Hope you have a wonderful time here. Hey, if you see in the paper (or my my website, www.mooseofhumor.com) that I'm nearby telling stories, stop by. Maybe you'll have a story or two of your own to tell. I'll introduce you to some genuine New Hampshire natives.

One other thing—you might want to double-check some of my "facts" before you go quoting them. I am a professional liar, after all.

Rock-Solid Resources

If you want more information about New Hampshire and insist that it be accurate, there are many good options. Many of the larger individual hotels, motels, restaurants, inns and attractions have their own websites. And here are a few sites that can help you plan a trip to the Granite State. You are on your own for UFO rides.

Websites

These websites were of great help to me as I compiled this book. You might find them helpful, too.

visitnh.gov

You're going to love it here! Information from the Department of Resources and Economic Development.

nh.com

An up-to-date listing of goings-on.

trainsnh.com

All the commercial train rides—more than you'd think.

wildlife.state.nh.us

The website for New Hampshire Fish and Game Department.

mountwashington.org

The view from the top of the state.

seacoastnh.com

J. Dennis Robinson's excellent website on all things current and historic on the seacoast.

nhmagazine.com

The essential guide to living in and visiting the Granite State.

Books

For more information about New Hamsphire or some of the things I have discussed in this book, please check out these books.

Boggis, JerriAnne with Eve Allegra Raimon and Barbara A. White, eds. *Harriet Wilson's New England: Race, Writing, and Region* (University of New Hampshire Press, 2007). Who says New Hampshire has no racial diversity? We do. And we always have. Harriet Wilson lived in Milford in the 1800s. This book tells the story of how she became the first African-American woman novelist. And what that means.

Cash, Kevin. *Who the Hell IS William Loeb?* (Amoskeag Press, 1975). The unauthorized biography of New Hampshire's most famous publisher and name-caller. Loeb's editorials would curl your hair. He made grown men cry, including presidential hopeful Ed Muskie—though Muskie claimed the wet on his face was just melting snowflakes.

Clayton, John. *You Know You're in New Hampshire When . . . .* (Insider's Guide, Globe Pequot, 2005). John Clayton, longtime columnist for the *Manchester Union Leader* knows New Hampshire like the keyboard on his computer.

dePaola, Tomie. *Front Porch Tales and North Country Whoppers* (Putnam, 2007). For older kids and adults, these are old Yankee stories from Maine, New Hampshire, and Vermont. Funny illustrations, too. You can order signed copies from the Morgan Hill Bookstore in New London. There's a link on www.tomie.com.

de Rham, Mickey. *Hey Bossie, You're a Spokescow!* (Plaidswede, 2004). A children's book about the celebrated Holstein with the Old Man of the Mountain on her shoulder.

Fuller, John. *The Interrupted Journey* (Berkley Medallion Books, 1966). True tale of alien abduction in the White Mountains. Believe!

Gardner, Kevin. *The Granite Kiss* (The Countryman Press, 2001). If you want to know all about stone walls and how to build them, read this book. Gardner's built a lot of walls in his lifetime. And he writes pretty, too.

Gregg, Hugh and Gardner, Bill. *Why? New Hampshire: The First-in-the-Nation Primary State* (Resources—New Hampshire, 2003). All you need to know about why New Hampshire is America's only choice for the first primary. Gregg, a Republican, and Gardner, a Democrat, regale readers with stories of the candidates, whether they're fringe, third-party, independent, mainstream, or gorillas.

Jones, Eric. *New Hampshire Curiosities* (Insider's Guide, Globe Pequot, 2006). This is a funny book full of real true actual facts.

Lawson, Russell. *Passaconaway's Realm: Captain John Evans and the Exploration of Mount Washington* (University Press of New England, 2002). Detailed history by a professor from Oklahoma.

Mandel, Norma H. *Beyond the Garden Gate: The Life of Celia Laighton Thaxter* (University Press of New England, 2004).

Mansfield, Howard, ed. *Where the Mountain Stands Alone: Stories of Place in the Monadnock Region* (University Press of New England, 2006).

McKenzie, Alexander. *The Way It Was: Mount Washington Observatory, 1934–1935* (A.A. Mckenzie, Publisher, 1994).

Michelson, Richard. Illustrated by Mary Azarian. *Tuttle's Red Barn: The Story of America's Oldest Family Farm* (G.P. Putnam's Sons, 2007).

Pagel, David, *The First Chinook: The Adventures of Arthur T. Walden and His Legendary Sled Dog, Chinook* (Kenspeckle Letterpress: 2005). This story about a miraculous but real dog rhymes! And it's illustrated with wood engravings by Rick Allen. My favorite dog book ever!

Perrault, John. *The Ballad of Louis Wagner and Other New England Stories in Verse* (Peter E. Randall Publisher, 2003). Besides the haunting and gory story of the double murder on Smuttynose in 1873, John includes lots of other ballads and poems, or, as we call them in the vernacular, "poims," many set in New Hampshire, with photographs to match taken by Peter Randall.

Pflock, Karl and Brookesmith, Peter, eds. *Encounters at Indian Head: The Betty and Barney Hill UFO Abduction Revisited.* (Anomalist Books, 2007). The story of Betty and Barney Hill and their alien encounter is one of the more bizarre in the long history of abductions, alien encounters, and UFO sightings in New Hampshire. Betty and Barney got up-close-and-personal with the nosy little bug-eyed buggers from another galaxy. We know it was another galaxy because Betty and Barney drew a map.

Saine, P. J. *New Hampshire Rock Portraits* (University Press of New England, 2004). This photographer sees things in rocks— 52 pictures of rocks. Some look like something other than rocks: eyes, smiles and profiles. Others look like rocks, but in unusual or artistic settings. He includes New Hampshire facts and quotes with his rock pictures.

Tardiff, Olive. *They Paved the Way—A History of New Hampshire Women* (Women for Women Weekly Press, 1980). The whole story of our witch, Goody Cole, and other remarkable women.

Tree, Christina and Hamm, Christine. *New Hampshire: An Explorer's Guide* (The Countryman Press, 2006). Very thorough and helpful.

Wallner, Peter A. *Franklin Pierce: New Hampshire's Favorite Son* (Plaidswede, 2004) and *Franklin Pierce: Martyr for the Union* (Plaidswede, 2007). This is hefty reading, but when you finish you'll know everything worth knowing about our 14th President. Some say he wa'n't that great a President. But, heck, he was up against it.

Williams, Thomas. *Leah, New Hampshire* (Morrow, 1992). One of my favorite collections of short stories, includes the classic "Horned Pout Are Evil," which they are.

Wood, Paula Casey. *The Barefoot Farmer of Pawtuckaway* (Revolution Books, 2007). George Goodrich wasn't exactly a hermit. But he and his wife, Susie, lived on a remote homestead in the hinterlands, now Pawtuckaway State Park. And he was a character—farmer, photographer, diarist, musician, and maker of fiddles and cellos. He didn't get into town much, but when he did he created a bit of a stir, especially among visitors, with his long hair and beard, his baggy overalls, and bare feet. Wood's small book includes photographs by and of George, a history of the family, and a glimpse of life in rural New Hampshire in the late 1800s and early 1900s. Yup, George was different. That's the way we like 'em.

About the Author

Rebecca Rule has lived in New Hampshire all her life (so far). She is a graduate of the University of New Hampshire and taught writing classes there for a number of years. She is the author of three short story collections about New Hampshire, including *The Best Revenge*—named Outstanding Work of Fiction by the New Hampshire Writers Project—and *Could Have Been Worse: True Stories, Embellishments and Outright Lies*. She is best known for her live storytelling events, many sponsored by the New Hampshire Humanities Council. She lives in Northwood with her husband, John, and wire fox terrier, Bob. She spends summers at Donnell Pond in Franklin, Maine.